Mark Hotchkiss is rare these days. For many years he has been thinking, researching, grappling with issues of philosophy and apologetics, for his own growth and benefit, and for others. In his manuscript *Legend of the Unknown God,* Mark presents with great clarity the results of his years of deliberation on the question of a logical reason for our faith. He has written, for both the thoughtful and open hearted, a book of importance to bolster faith and prepare us for greater effectiveness with those we share Christ with. It is a delight for me to endorse this work, and recommend it to the reader as a book of substance and blessing.

Dr. Stan DeKoven
President
Vision International University

■ ■ ■

Mark Hotchkiss is a man who has come from a solid spiritual root. He is a modern day "Berean" Christian who searches out a matter to not only see whether it is true or not, but also to provide context and unfold deeper understandings and insights. Mark is not afraid to delve into all that God's Word and history teaches about an era to help shed light on what we know from Scripture. The *Legend of the Unknown God* is an unusual manuscript that Mark has written. He explains the historical context into which the Apostle Paul was preaching in Athens when the Greeks brought him to the Areopagus and demanded to know more about the new religion he was preaching about. Mark then traces back several centuries of history to give a reader a fascinating journey into the culture and context of that region of the world. When it is all said and done, Paul's reference to the "Unknown God" makes a whole lot more sense.

Dr. Berin Gilfillan
Founder: International School of Ministry

■ ■ ■

It is with great pleasure that I write this endorsement of the excellent book by Mark Hotchkiss, *Legend of the Unknown God*. From the time that I opened the first page I was enthralled with it and unable to put it down. It revolutionized my impressions of the ancient biblical texts I had studied all of my life, and gave me a new appreciation for the ancient biblical kings and queens who shaped the religious experience that we herald today. I learned so much about Socrates and his protégé Plato, and the key roles they played in biblical history for which they never received adequate credit. Thanks to Mark, the ancient times of Jewish history came to life for me. When I read the recent Associated Press news article entitled "Saving Babylon: Can this ancient city located in Iraq be rescued?" I thought about this book and the way in which Mark chronicled the many episodes of God's plan unfolding in this great city of our world, our past and ultimately our future. May God bless the reading of this work that it may inspire many to seek deeper into

His word and grow eternally thereby. And may He bless you to write many more epics that further explore the true historical backdrops of the characters of the Bible we have come to read about, know and love.

Respectfully submitted,
Veronica A. Wilkerson Johnson, M.A., Director
University of Michigan Lansing Service Center

■ ■ ■

I have had the privilege of reading the *Legend of the Unknown God* in its manuscript form, and I found it most enjoyable. Not only from the perspective of History, of which I'm an avid student of, but also the Scriptural insight, study, and research put into this project. I thoroughly appreciated the full circle and completion of the book. It is very well written and thought out. Whether you're a student of history, historical literature, or even just Greek history and philosophy, this is a must read.

Dominic Garrisi
Radio Broadcast Engineer / Bible College Student
Gaylord, MI

■ ■ ■

Legend of the Unknown God is a compelling must read for both laypersons and committed students of Biblical Ancient History. Marks omni-present perspective of characters depicted in the telling of historical times and events of kings is insightful and educational. The point of view in Marks work places one at the scene of ancient events, and makes one privy to plausible conversations as if present. We, the readers of *Legend of the Unknown God* are the proverbial flies on the walls of kings, or on the garments of those who speak. We are made witness to the hopes, fears and schemes of various characters as history is revealed.

Maurice Davison
Photographer, Lansing Michigan

Legend of the Unknown God

Legend of the Unknown God

by Mark A. Hotchkiss

TATE PUBLISHING & *Enterprises*

Published by Tate Publishing & Enterprises, LLC
127 E. Trade Center Terrace | Mustang, Oklahoma 73064 USA
1.888.361.9473 | www.tatepublishing.com

Tate Publishing is committed to excellence in the publishing industry. The company reflects the philosophy established by the founders, based on Psalm 68:11,
"The Lord gave the word and great was the company of those who published it."

Book design copyright © 2009 by Tate Publishing, LLC. All rights reserved.
Cover design by Tyler Evans
Cover photo by Amanda B. Hotchkiss
Interior design by Stephanie Woloszyn

Published in the United States of America

ISBN: 978-1-60696-679-2
1. Religion
2. Christian/History
09.04.27

Table
of Contents

Foreword

It is with great pleasure I put my hand to this task. Years have passed since meeting the Hotchkiss family. Young Mark has taken me on this journey through the Old Testament like no other writer. Most of the information we have is handed down from generation to generation. Mark has combined the current information available through new research of world history with what we know about the Old Testament.

Down through history God has inspired men to dig into the facts. Through digging, we have many of the truths that support the doctrines we hold to in Christendom today. God, through the Holy Spirit, has inspired men to dig deeper than the generation preceding them.

Mark had some questions, which in his mind needed to be answered. Through hours and hours of research, prayer, and study, God has given him this message. He has shared those answers in this book so that we may all benefit from what God has shown to him.

Purpose is the pick and shovel that enabled Mark Hotchkiss to accomplish such a momentous task. This book gives the reader the opportunity to gain a deeper understanding of the events and times of the Bible. It asks us to consider our own knowledge of who we worship. But most importantly it cries out to a nation that is bound to repeat history: "Turn back to God." In reading this book, you will experience the depth of the mine from which knowledge came to the surface.

Dr. C.D. Tyler, Founder,
Victory World Missions International Ministries

Introduction

This book is written in three phases. The first is a philosophical aspect. For those readers that love philosophy, I have a surprise for you. In Acts chapter 17, Paul is in Athens talking to the philosophers of the day. He mentions the Alter that was inscribed "To an Unknown God." This is the source for the title of this book. That Alter was there for a reason and this book will make a suggestion of how that Alter came about.

This takes us to the second phase, a historical look from the Jewish exile to the last days of the prophets around 400 BC. In order to discover the source of the Alter this book will take the reader on a historical trip. This trip will discover how Judaism migrated to Athens so that Paul could claim that the Athenians were worshiping the Living God but did not know it. For those readers that love history, you will find some added knowledge from a perspective not seen in the Old Testament. I have grown up reading about Daniel, Shadrach, Meshach, Abednego, Esther, and the others. I loved these stories, but I never looked at them from the perspectives of the Babylonian and Persian kings. This book takes into consideration the archeological artifacts that were found, left by these ancient kings that tell some of the same stories, but from their point of view. These artifacts add historical information not found in the Old Testament. This new information only strengthens my faith in the Bible and convinces me that the information is in fact true.

The third phase is theological. I want you, the reader, to evaluate whether you actually know what God you are worshiping. Are you like the Athenians, not knowing who you are worshipping? There is a saying that goes, "If we don't learn from history, we are bound to repeat it." Are we as a nation following in the footsteps of the Israelites and turning our back on God, worshiping a god of our lifestyle? Will we as a nation find ourselves servants to a foreign nation like the Israelites did? I believe everyone needs to evaluate where they are with God and how they worship Him. I pray that as you read this book you will gain an understanding of the reality and emphasis that God places on our worship of Him. It is my hope that we as a nation can turn our worship back to God and avoid the same punishment that befell the Israelites, a life of servitude to a pagan nation.

Paul
of Tarsus

The "Hill of Ares," northwest of the Acropolis, once functioned as the chief homicide court of Athens. It is now used to investigate corruption. One day, a group of Epicurean and Stoic philosophers happened to be disputing in the market place. Their philosophies of life being so different, they often argued of these things.

One could understand the Stoic philosophy simplest by understanding the character of Spock on the popular television show *Star Trek*. Stoic ethics teach freedom from passion by following reason. They did not seek to eliminate emotions. They only wanted to avoid emotional troubles by developing clear judgment and inner calm through diligent practice of logic, reflection, and concentration.

The Epicurean philosophers propounded an ethic of individual pleasure as the sole or chief good in life. The Epicureans were as close to atheism as they could get without actually denying the existence of the gods. They sought the greatest amount of pleasure possible during one's lifetime, yet to do so moderately in order to avoid the suffering incurred by overindulgence in such pleasure. Today they have found a new subject to taunt: Paul of Tarsus. Tarsus is a city on the other side of the Aegean

Sea, in Asia Minor. Paul is discussing the newest religious belief, Christianity. He is a follower of the Jewish man, Jesus, executed by the Romans at the request of the Jews. The philosophers asked, "What is this babbler trying to say?" Others would remark, "He seems to be advocating foreign gods" (Acts 17:18, NIV).

Athens is a powerful city-state, a center for the arts, learning and philosophy; the birthplace of democracy. It was once said that Athens had more gods than men. These men of Athens did not take kindly to strangers that disrupted their thoughts of religion, especially those that spoke of a God greater than their own. Although they were intrigued by the latest ideas, an attack on the gods was dangerous, a subject considered to be a corruptible offense.

It is perhaps misleading to speak of "Greek religion." In the first place, the Greeks did not have a term for "religion" in the sense of a dimension of existence distinct from all others, and grounded in the belief that the gods exercise authority over the fortunes of human beings and demand recognition as a condition for salvation. The Greeks spoke of their religious doings as things having to do with the gods, but this loose usage did not imply the existence of any authoritative set of "beliefs." Indeed, the Greeks did not have a word for "belief" in either of the two senses familiar to us. Since the existence of the gods was a given, it would have made no sense to ask whether someone "believed" that the gods existed. On the other hand, individuals could certainly show themselves to be more or less mindful of the gods, but the common term for that possibility is simply "customary." It was their "custom" to acknowledge the gods and their rightful place in the scheme of things, and to act accordingly by giving them their due. Some bold individuals could observe the customs of the gods, but deny that they were due some of the customary observances. But these customary observances were so highly unsystematic that it is not easy to describe the ways in which they were normal for anyone.

Today people customize God to fit their lifestyles and they do not actually give God his rightful dues. People today just go through the motions without any real commitment or understanding. There is such a wide variety of customary observances today with which we confuse ourselves, and again, just as with the Greeks, it is not easy to describe the ways in which they are normal for anyone.

The men of Athens took Paul to the Areopagus, where they could determine if charges of corruption could be introduced. They said to him, "May we know what this new teaching is that you are presenting? You are bringing some strange ideas to our ears, and we want to know what they mean" (Acts 17:19–20, NIV). It's not certain whether they actually wanted to know, or if they wanted to catch Paul in a situation so that they could bring charges against him.

> Paul stood up in the Areopagus and said; Men of Athens! I see that in every way you are very religious. For as I walked around and looked carefully at your objects of worship, I have even found an altar with this inscription: 'To an Unknown God.' Now what

> you worship as something unknown I am going to proclaim to you.
>
> Acts 17:22–23 (NIV) }

Paul had found a loophole, for he was a wise man and anointed by God. The God he wanted to introduce to the Greeks was the true "Living God." He was, of course, referring to the God of Abraham, the God of the Jews. By using the altar "To an Unknown God," he is not introducing a "new" God to the Greeks; he is explaining the God that they are already worshiping but do not know.

This was not the first time that this "Unknown God," this "Living God," the God of the Jews, was introduced to the Greeks in Athens. It is also not the first time that the Greeks have taken someone to the Areopagus for introducing a new divinity to them. But this story starts long before Paul ever arrived, going back more than 700 years to a time when the Greek people did not exist under the name "Greeks" and the country name of "Greece" was not used. They called their land "Hellas" and themselves "Hellenes." At first the word "Hellas" signified only a small district in Thessaly, from which the Hellenes gradually spread over the whole country. The names "Greece" and "Greeks" came to us from the Romans, who gave the name "Graecia" to the country and "Graeci" to the inhabitants. (For the sake of familiarity, Greece will refer to the area and Greeks will refer to the inhabitants.)

A Good Place to Start

In the sixth and seventh century BC, the nobles of the Greek territories (Attica), control the government through a membership known as the Areopagus. This is a council which takes its name from the hill of Ares where they meet. The council chooses seven members of nobility annually to serve as "archons." These seven men conduct the business of both government and law. They serve for one year and then become members of the Areopagus for life. The middle-class citizens take part in an assembly known as the ecclesia, but their role is minor. The government would change over time, with Oligarchs and tyrants, until it becomes a democracy in the late fifth century BC.

The eighth century BC through the fifth century BC was a time of prophets and prophetic messages in a land far from the Greeks. The people of Israel and Judah were turning against the ways of their fathers. They were building altars and temples to foreign gods and worshiping them. The God of their fathers was a jealous God and was sending messages to them through the prophets. The prophets would receive a message straight from God and tell whomever God instructed them to tell. In Greece, the Greeks did not speak to, or receive messages directly from, their gods. They would go to the temple of the Oracle and pay a price, after which the Oracle (a young female, in an induced trance) would mumble a message that would be interpreted by the priests in the temple. Most times the message would be ambiguous at best. There were many prophets throughout the history of Judah and Israel, but there would come a time when there would be no more, a day of the last prophet of the Living God.

Around 766 BC, a time after the nation of Israel had split into two kingdoms, the kingdom of Israel (to the north) and the kingdom of Judah (to the south), Menahem became the king of the kingdom of Israel, but the Israelites had fallen to the anger of God. The prophet Isaiah was God's voice, warning the Israelites to turn away from false gods, idols, and sorcery. They did not listen to Isaiah and continued in their ways. God sent the Assyrian King Tiglath-Pileser to invade their land. King Tiglath-Pileser was not a man without a price; King Menahem bought off the Assyrian king with gold and silver. But this would not be the last that Israel would see of King Tiglath-Pileser.

After Menahem's reign, his son Pekahiah would take the throne, but for only two years. He was assassinated by about fifty men of Gilead, lead by Pekah. Pekah would succeed Pekahiah as king of Israel, but it was not a peaceful reign. It was around 734 BC/732 BC, during Pekah's reign, when King Tiglath-Pileser once again showed his face and invaded the northern territories of the Israeli kingdom. This time he deported its inhabitants to Assyria and claimed the land for the Assyrian Empire.

Not wishing to take on the Assyrian king, Pekah made an alliance with Rezin, king of Aram, and turns his attention to his brothers in the south. Together Pekah and Rezin began to make trouble with the kings of Judah, Jotham and his successor Ahaz. During the reign of Ahaz, Pekah and Rezin besieged Jerusalem but could not overpower Ahaz.

> Ahaz appealed to King Tiglath-Pileser king of Assyria, "I am your servant and vassal. Come up and save me out of the hand of the king of Aram and of the king of Israel, who are attacking me." Ahaz paid off Tiglath with silver and gold, so Tiglath attacked Damascus and captured it. He deported its inhabitants and executed Rezin.
>
> II Kings 16:7 (NIV)

Around 727 BC, King Tiglath-Pileser was succeeded by his son Shalmaneser V and in 726 BC, Hoshea became king of Israel. Hoshea followed his father's example by worshiping idols and false gods. He also continued his dislike for the Assyrian King Shalmaneser V. The agreement between the Assyrians and the Israelites was simple to understand. All Hoshea was asked to do was to accept Shalmaneser as his overlord and pay him a tribute. For this, Shalmaneser agreed to let Hoshea continue as king over Israel. In modern days, we would call that a "protection fee." Hoshea's solution to a bad situation was to befriend his enemy's enemy, the king of Egypt. Shalmaneser discovered that Hoshea had betrayed him by hooking up with the king of Egypt, and no longer paid him the tribute. The simple solution was that he seized Hoshea and put him in prison, invaded Israel and captured its capital Samaria around 722 BC. He deported the inhabitants to Assyria and brought people from the Assyrian cities such as Babylon, Cuthah, Ava, Hamath, and Sepharvaim to settle in Samaria and replace the Israelites. This act of rebellion establishes the existence of the Israelites in the northern region of Assyria and begins the movement of Judaism, the worship of the living God, toward the Greeks.

Back in Samaria, the new inhabitants realized that something was wrong. There were lions entering the city and killing them off. The gods they were worshiping did not protect them and they decided that it must have been the God of the Israelites that sent in the lions. They reported to the king of Assyria: "The people you deported and resettled in the towns of Samaria do not know what the God of that country requires. He has sent lions among them, which are killing them off, because the people do not know what he requires" (II Kings 17:26, NIV).

The king of Assyria gave the order to have a priest of the Israelites return to Samaria and teach the people how to properly worship the Living God. He said, "Have one of the priests you took captive from Samaria go back to live there and teach the people what the God of the land requires" (II Kings 17:27, NIV). So, one of the priests who had been exiled from Samaria went back to teach them how to worship the Lord. Even though they worshiped the Lord, they also served their own gods in accordance with the customs of the nations from which they had been brought. These people became known as the Samaritans.

Judah Follows in Israel's Footsteps

Around 640 BC in the kingdom of Judah, when Josiah was placed on the throne by the "People of the Land," at the age of 8, the international situation was in flux: to the east, the Assyrian Empire was in the beginning stages of its eventual disintegration, the Babylonian Empire had not yet arose to replace it, and Egypt to the west was still recovering from Assyrian rule. In this power vacuum, Jerusalem was able to govern itself without foreign intervention. But, in 627 BC, the thirteenth year of Josiah's rule, a prophet named Jeremiah began to receive the word of the Lord. Jeremiah tells Josiah that God has compared Judah to Israel and says that "Faithless Israel is more righteous than unfaithful Judah" (Jeremiah 3:11, NIV). The warnings are made; however, Josiah ignores Jeremiah. God gave them an opportunity to turn back to him and end their idol worship. Because they ignored Him, God raises up a conqueror against them. It is at this time that the Babylonian, Nabopolassar, rose up and revolted against the Assyrian Empire and regained a stronghold for the Babylonians, claiming the throne of the Neo-Babylonian Empire.

In the eighteenth year of Josiah's rule, 622 BC, the Jewish book of laws was re-discovered in the Temple in Jerusalem. Josiah discovered that his father, Amon, and his grandfather, Manasseh, the kings before him, had allowed the people to turn from God and worship idols and foreign gods, practice sorcery and divination, and consult mediums and spiritists. He had been raised with these practices and they seemed normal to him, much the same as modern times. As the years pass and people allow more ungodly practices to occur, they become normal and are accepted by each new generation. Josiah's eyes were opened up when he read the Jewish book of laws. He realized they were no longer following God. They had created false gods, were practicing blasphemous acts and they needed to turn back to God. Josiah feared God's judgment through the warnings of Jeremiah. As a result, he renewed the covenant between the kingdom of Judah and God; "nevertheless, the LORD did not turn away from the heat of his fierce anger, which burned against Judah because of all that Manasseh had done to provoke him to anger" (II Kings 23:26, NIV). The kingdom of Judah was not off the hook; but, Josiah, because of his obedience, was spared from witnessing the destruction of Judah. During the rest of his reign, the kingdom of Judah was under a period of grace, which did not continue after Josiah's death because his successors did not continue to honor God. Jeremiah continued to prophesy and give warning, but it was to no avail.

Over the years, Assyria and Egypt made an alliance while Nabopolassar made a strong ally with the king of the Median Empire, Cyaxares. The Princess of Mede, Amytis, was given to the Prince of Babylon, Nebuchadnezzar, as his bride. Around 609 BC, Pharaoh Necho II, king of Egypt, went up to the Euphrates River to help the king of Assyria against Nabopolassar, king of Babylon, and his ally the Medes. There is a great power struggle between these empires. Assyria was to the north of Judah, Egypt was to the southwest, Babylon and the Median Empire were to the east. It would not be in King Josiah's best interest to allow Assyria and Egypt to completely surround him, considering the fact that it was Egypt that enslaved the Jewish people for more than 400 years. It was Assyria that conquered the kingdom of Israel and exiled them from their land. It was not a tough choice to make. Josiah made the decision to assist Nabopolassar against the Egyptian army and marched out to meet Pharaoh Necho II in battle, if only to delay the Egyptian army. Necho II faced Josiah and killed him at Megiddo. Josiah's servants brought his body in a chariot from the battle fields of Megiddo to Jerusalem and buried him. Jehoahaz, son of Josiah, was anointed king in place of his father, at the age of twenty-three. Nabopolassar destroyed the remnants of the Assyrian Empire with the help of the Medes and continued to wage war against Egypt for the next four years. Having conquered the Assyrian Empire and claiming the land, there are now people worshiping the "Living God," throughout the new Babylonian Empire.

In Judah, Jehoahaz reigned for only three months and "he did evil in the eyes of the Lord" (II Kings 23:32, NIV). Pharaoh Necho II was not happy with the people of Judah, for the obvious reason that they delayed him; therefore, he put Jehoahaz in chains at Riblah in the land of Hamath, where Necho II set up his camp in preparations to fight the Babylonians for the next four years. He then imposed on Judah a levy of a hundred talents of silver and a talent of gold to help fund his army. Needing a ruler in Judah that would accept him as their overlord, Pharaoh Necho II made Eliakim, brother of Jehoahaz and son of Josiah, the vassal king and changed Eliakim's name to Jehoiakim, around 609 BC. Egypt continued their march to the Euphrates to wage war against the Babylonians, even though the Assyrian army had already been beaten. Jehoiakim was a good puppet and paid Pharaoh Necho II the silver and gold he demanded to fund the war. In order to do so, he taxed the land and exacted the silver and gold from the people of the land according to their assessments.

In the face of the heavy tax burden, Jehoiakim had lavish palaces built with forced labor. Jeremiah cried out:

> Woe to him who builds his palace by unrighteousness, his upper rooms by injustice, making his countrymen work for nothing, not paying them for their labor. He says, "I will build myself a great palace with spacious upper rooms." So he makes large windows in it, panels it with cedar and decorates it in red.
>
> Jeremiah 22:13–14 (NIV)

Jehoiakim enthusiastically practiced idol worship and the sins associated with it. The people "… built the high places of Baal to burn their sons in the fire as offerings to Baal" (Jeremiah 19:5, NIV). God sent the prophets Urijah and Jeremiah to expose Jehoiakim's sins, but Jehoiakim had Urijah killed and Jeremiah was persecuted. Jeremiah dictated his prophesies to Baruch, who wrote them down in a scroll and circulated it around the city. Jehoiakim burned the scroll and tried to imprison Jeremiah and Baruch, but they had escaped. Jeremiah, having heard the scroll had been burned, wrote another one. This time he added:

> This is what the LORD says about Jehoiakim king of Judah: He will have no one to sit on the throne of David; his body will be thrown out and exposed to the heat by day and the frost by night. I will punish him and his children and his attendants for their wickedness; I will bring on them and those living in Jerusalem and the people of Judah every disaster I pronounced against them, because they have not listened.
>
> Jeremiah 36:30–31 (NIV)

Nebuchadnezzar

In 606 BC, the war between the Babylonians and the Egyptians had been going on for three years. Nebuchadnezzar realized that the best wayto defeat the Egyptians was to cut off their finances used to fund the war; so he decided to attack Jerusalem. This was prophesied by Jeremiah, and Judah was conquered. Nebuchadnezzar took articles of gold from the temple and carried them off to Babylon. It was at this time that many Jews, including Daniel with his three companions, Shadrach, Meshach, and Abednego, were exiled to Babylon. This was the third year of Jehoiakim.[1]

It was in 605 BC, "…in the fourth year of Jehoiakim son of Josiah king of Judah" (Jeremiah 46:2), that Nebuchadnezzar prince to the throne of Babylon won the battle of Carchemish against the Egyptian Pharaoh Necho II. He ascended to the throne of Babylon shortly thereafter when his father Nabopolassar died.[2]

In 601 BC, Nebuchadnezzar was faced with rebellion by Jehoiakim and he returned to Jerusalem to set the matter straight. This time, leaving Jehoiakim on his throne in Jerusalem, he treated him as a vassal king. This position lasted for only three years: "…Jehoiakim became his vassal for three years, but then he changed his mind and rebelled against Nebuchadnezzar" (2 Kings 24:1, NIV). Again, Nebuchadnezzar returned to Jerusalem, but this time Jehoiakim is killed and his son, Jehoiachin, takes the throne. Jehoiakim reigned in Jerusalem for a total of eleven years, until 598 BC, the seventh year of Nebuchadnezzar's reign as king.[3] There is confusion between the "Jerusalem Chronicles" and the Bible. The Jerusalem Chronicles say that Nebuchadnezzar invaded Jerusalem in his seventh year, but the Bible says it was his eighth year. There has been no explanation for this, but one will be offered now. In the book of Daniel, it says:

> In the third year of the reign of Jehoiakim king of Judah, Nebuchadnezzar king of Babylon came to Jerusalem and besieged it.

This is where the date of 606 BC is found, the third year of Jehoiakim.

In the book of Jeremiah, it says:

> This is the message against the army of Pharaoh Necho II king of Egypt, which was defeated at Carchemish on the Euphrates River by Nebuchadnezzar king of Babylon in the fourth year of Jehoiakim son of Josiah king of Judah.
>
> Jeremiah 46:2 (NIV)

The fourth year of Jehoiakim, 605 BC, was the year Nebuchadnezzar defeated Egypt at the Battle of Carchemish. Nebuchadnezzar did not ascend to the throne of Babylon until after this battle. This is one year after the author of the book of Daniel (assumed to be Daniel) has referred to Nebuchadnezzar as "king." It is not then a surprise to see that the Israelites would say "the eighth year of Nebuchadnezzar" while the Jerusalem Chronicles would say "seventh." The Israelites saw Nebuchadnezzar as the "ruler" of Babylon, and referred to him as "king." It would appear that this error is corrected in the second chapter of Daniel. In the first chapter, Daniel is taken to Babylon to serve in the palace.

> Then the king ordered Ashpenaz, chief of his court officials, to bring in some of the Israelites from the royal family and the nobility–young men without any physical defect, handsome, showing aptitude for every kind of learning, well-informed, quick to understand, and qualified to serve in the king's palace. He was to teach them the language and literature of the Babylonians. The king assigned them a daily amount of food and wine from the king's table. They were to be trained for three years, and after that they were to enter the king's service.
>
> Daniel 1:3–5 (NIV)

He and the others were to be trained for three years before entering the king's service. In the second chapter of Daniel, it says:

> In the second year of his reign, Nebuchadnezzar had dreams; his mind was troubled and he could not sleep.
>
> Daniel 2:1 (NIV)

It is at this time that we see Daniel and the others in the king's service among the wise men of Babylon, the Chaldean Magi. By doing the math, Nebuchadnezzar's second year of reign plus the one year before, puts Daniel and the others at three years of training prior to entering the king's service.

The confusion; therefore, could possibly be that the Israelites are referring to Nebuchadnezzar as the Babylonian "ruler" and call him "king."

In any case, the city of Jerusalem was besieged and defeated in 598 BC, as the prophet Jeremiah warned:

> Jehoiachin king of Judah, his mother, his attendants, his nobles and his officials all surrendered to him ... In the eighth year of the reign of the king of Babylon, he took Jehoiachin prisoner. As the LORD had declared, Nebuchadnezzar removed all the treasures from the temple of the LORD and from the royal palace, and took away all the gold articles that Solomon king of Israel had made for the temple of the LORD. He carried into exile all Jerusalem: all the officers and fighting men, and all the craftsmen and artisans—a total of ten thousand. Only the poorest people of the land were left.

> Nebuchadnezzar took Jehoiachin captive to Babylon. He also took from Jerusalem to Babylon the king's mother, his wives, his officials and the leading men of the land. The king of Babylon also deported to Babylon the entire force of seven thousand fighting men, strong and fit for war, and a thousand craftsmen and artisans. He made Mattaniah, Jehoiachin's uncle, king in his place and changed his name to Zedekiah.
>
> 2 Kings 24:12–17 (NIV)

Jeremiah wrote a letter to the exiles and priests that were carried off into Babylon. He instructed them:

> Build houses and settle down; plant gardens and eat what they produce. Marry and have sons and daughters; find wives for your sons and give your daughters in marriage, so that they too may have sons and daughters. Increase in number there; do not decrease. Also, seek the peace and prosperity of the city to which the Lord has carried you into exile. Pray to the Lord for it, because if it prospers, you too will prosper.
>
> Jeremiah 29:5–7 (NIV)

It was early in the reign of Zedekiah that the Lord instructed the prophet Jeremiah to send this message to Zedekiah king of Judah, and to the kings of Edom, Moab, Ammon, Tyre and Sidon:

With my great power and outstretched arm I made the earth and its people and the animals that are on it, and I give it to anyone I please. Now I will hand all your countries over to my servant Nebuchadnezzar king of Babylon; I will make even the wild animals subject to him. All nations will serve him and his son and his grandson until the time for his land comes; then many nations and great kings will subjugate him.

Jeremiah 27:5–7 (NIV)

In the ninth year of Zedekiah's reign, Nebuchadnezzar king of Babylon marched against Jerusalem with his whole army. He encamped outside the city and built siege works all around it. The city was kept under siege until the eleventh year of King Zedekiah, [586 BC]. By the ninth day of the fourth month the famine in the city had become so severe that there was no food for the people to eat. Then the city wall was broken through, and the whole army fled at night through the gate between the two walls near the king's garden, though the Babylonians were surrounding the city. They fled toward the Arabah [Jordan Valley], but the Babylonian army pursued the king and overtook him in the plains of Jericho. All his soldiers were separated from him and scattered, and he was captured. He was taken to the king of Babylon at Riblah, where sentence was pronounced on him. They killed the sons of

Zedekiah before his eyes. Then they put out his eyes, bound him with bronze shackles and took him to Babylon.

2 Kings 25:1–7 (NIV)

Nebuchadnezzar instructed his commander, Nebuzaradan, to set fire to the temple of the Lord, the royal palace at Jerusalem and all the houses. Every important building was burned down. Then the whole Babylonian army, under the commander of the imperial guard, broke down the walls around Jerusalem and carried into exile the people who remained. But again, they left behind some of the poorest people of the land to work the vineyards and fields.[4]

The city of Jerusalem had been destroyed, the people of Judah were exiled in Babylon, the people of Israel that were exiled to Assyria were in the northern territory of Babylonia the Chaldean Empire (Neo-Babylonian Empire), and the Living God was being worshiped in a foreign land. God's wrath had fallen upon the nations of Israel and Judah for their disobedience to his laws. They found a short period of grace because of Josiah's obedience and his renewal of the covenant, but Josiah's sons did not continue to honor the covenant and they did not heed the warnings of God's prophet. They returned to the sin that brought about God's anger.

The empires that existed at this time were: Lydian, Median, Chaldean (Neo-Babylonian), and Egyptian.

The Lord's promise to Zedekiah was coming true,

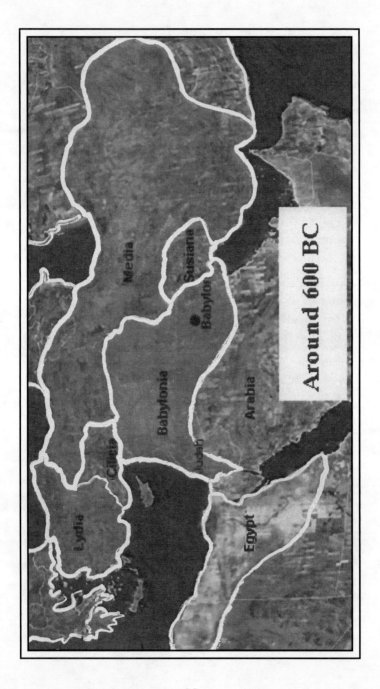

as Jeremiah had prophesied: "All nations will serve him (Nebuchadnezzar) and his son and his grandson until the time for his land comes; then many nations and great kings will subjugate him" (Jeremiah 27:7, NIV).

The prophet Jeremiah prophesied to all the people and the kings of Judah and the Levant region, telling them what the Lord God had instructed, and each time the prophesies were fulfilled. Jeremiah was not carried off to Babylon with the others, but instead stayed in Jerusalem with Gedaliah Ben Ahikam, the newly appointed governor of Jerusalem. Gedaliah was assassinated a few months later.[5]

In Babylon, four young men, Daniel (Belteshazzar), Hananiah (Shadrach), Mishael (Meshach), and Azariah (Abednego), are among a group brought before King Nebuchadnezzar to serve in the King's palace. Three years after their arrival, around 603 BC, the king has a dream that he does not understand. He orders all the wise men of Babylon, the Chaldean Magi, to tell him his dream and the meaning of it. None are able to do this except Daniel. Daniel finds favor in the king's eyes by fulfilling the king's command. He tells the king what his dream was, and the meaning of it. Daniel gives credit to the Living God the God of Abraham.[6]

Because the king is pleased with Daniel:

> The king said to Daniel, "Surely your God is the God of gods and the Lord of kings and a revealer of mysteries, for you were able to reveal this mystery." Then the king placed Daniel in a

> high position and lavished many gifts on him. He made him ruler over the entire province of Babylon and placed him in charge of all its wise men (the Chaldean Magi). Moreover, at Daniel's request the king appointed Shadrach, Meshach and Abednego administrators over the province of Babylon, while Daniel himself remained at the royal court.
>
> Daniel 2:47–49 (NIV)

Some time later, Shadrach, Meshach, and Abednego defied King Nebuchadnezzar's order that they bow down and worship a golden idol, a cult image of Nebuchadnezzar. Nebuchadnezzar, in a rage, orders the boys thrown into a furnace, but they are miraculously unharmed by the flames and survive the experience unscathed. Nebuchadnezzar sees them walking around in the furnace along with an unnamed fourth figure. After the three youths emerge, Nebuchadnezzar orders everyone to worship their God instead of the golden idol.[7]

Because of these four men and their trust and faith in the Living God the Babylonian Empire now worships the God of Abraham.

Cyrus

Keeping the lineage straight, Cyaxares was the father of Astyages. Astyages was the father of Mandané. Mandané was the mother of Cyrus. It was around 580/575 BC that a baby was born in the country north of Babylonia. The baby's name was Cyrus, the future king and redeemer of the Jewish people in Babylon as prophesied by Isaiah[8] almost 125 years earlier. His birth and early life is one of myth and legend and is told by the Greek historian Herodotus:

Astyages king of the Medes had a daughter whose name was Mandané; and of this daughter, when she was but a child, he dreamed such a dream that he feared exceedingly what might happen to him and to his kingdom by reason of her. Therefore when she grew of age to be married, he gave her not to a man of her own race, but he gave her to a Persian, whose name was Cambyses. And this Cambyses was indeed of a noble house, but of a quiet and peaceable temper. Only because he was a Persian, Astyages held him to be of less account than a Mede, whether he were noble or no.

But in the first year of the marriage King Astyages dreamed another dream of his daughter, which made him yet more afraid than had the former dream. Therefore he sent for the woman, who was now about to bring forth her first-born child, and kept her in the palace, being minded to put to death that which should be born of her, for the interpreters of dreams had signified to him that the son of his daughter should be king in his stead. When therefore she bare Cyrus, for they gave this name to the child, Astyages called to him one Harpagus, who was of his kindred, and faithful to him beyond all other of the Medes, and who had also the care of his household. And when Harpagus was come to him, the King said, "Harpagus, see thou that in the matter which I shall now put in thy charge thou in no wise neglect my commandment, nor prefer others to me, and so in the end bring great sorrow on thyself. Now the matter is this. Thou shalt take this child that Mandané my daughter hath lately borne, and carry it to thy home, and there slay it; and afterwards thou shalt bury it in such fashion as thou wilt."

To this Harpagus said, "O King, thou hast never perceived any transgression in thy servant in time past; and he will take good heed that he sin not against thee in time to come. And as for this matter of which thou speakest, if thou wilt have it so, it must needs be done."

When Harpagus had said this, they gave him the child into his hands, the child being dressed as if for death and burial, and he took it and went to his home weeping. And when he was come thither he said to his wife all the words that King Astyages had said to him. Then the woman spake, saying, "What then art thou minded to do in this matter?"

And he said, "Of a surety I shall not do as the King hath commanded me. For though he should be turned aside to folly, and be stricken with madness even more grievously than he is now stricken, yet why should I be the slayer of this child? And the causes wherefore I will not do this thing are many. For first he is of my own kindred, and next Astyages is an old man and hath no male offspring. If then when he shall die, his kingdom shall go to his daughter, whose child he biddeth me to slay, surely I shall stand in great peril. It must needs be that the child die; for how else shall I escape, but the slayer shall be one of the servants of Astyages, and not I or one of my own servants."

When he had thus spoken, he sent a messenger straightway to one of the herdsmen of Astyages, knowing that the man dwelt in a place well fitted for the purpose, that is to say, a mountain abounding in wild beasts. The name of this herdsman was Mitradates, and his wife was a slave woman, Spaco by name. As for the pastures where he pastured his herd, they lay under the mountains which are northwards from Ecbatana, towards the Black Sea. For this region of the land of Media is covered with woods and mountains, but the country for the most part is a plain country. The herdsman therefore being thus called came with all speed. And when he was come, Harpagus said to him, "Astyages bids thee take this child and put him in some desert place among the mountains that he may speedily perish. And he bids me say that if thou slay him not, but in any way sufferest him to live, he will destroy thee most miserably. And I am appointed to see that this thing be done."

When the herdsman heard these words he took the child and went on his way to his home, and came to the stalls of the cattle. Now it chanced that his wife had been in travail all that day, and that she bore a child while the herdsman was at the city. And the two were much troubled each about the other; for the husband feared lest haply it should go ill with his wife in her travail, and the woman was afraid because Harpagus had sent for her husband in much haste, which thing he had not been wont to do.

When therefore he had returned, the woman, seeing that he was come back speedily and beyond her hope, asked of him, saying, "Why did Harpagus send for thee in such haste?"

Then the man made answer, "When I was come to the city I saw and heard such things as I would had never befallen my masters; for the whole house of Harpagus was full of weeping and wailing. And when I went into the house, being sore astonished at these things, I saw a child lying there and crying; and the child was adorned with gold and fine clothing. And Harpagus, so soon as he saw me, bade me take up the child with all haste and depart, and put it on such mountain as I knew to be most haunted by wild beasts. And he said that King Astyages had given commandment that this should be done. And he added many threats of what should befall me, if I should not do as he had bidden me. Wherefore I took the child, and carried it away, thinking that it was the child of some one in the household; for the truth, as it was, I could not have imagined, yet did I marvel to see that the child was adorned with gold and fine apparel, and also that there should be so great a mourning in the house of Harpagus. But as I went on my way, one of the servants of Harpagus, whom he had sent with me, recounted to me the whole matter, that this child was the son of Mandané the daughter of Astyages and Cambyses the son of Cyrus, and that Astyages had given commandment that it should be slain. This therefore is the child whom thou seest."

And when the herdsman had said this he took away the covering, and showed the child to his wife. And when she saw the babe, that it was fair and well-favoured, she wept, and laid hold of her husband by his knees and besought him that he would not do this thing, putting forth the child to die. But the man answered that he could not by any means do otherwise, for that Harpagus would send those who would see whether the thing had been done or no, and that he should perish miserably if he should be found to have transgressed the commandment.

Then the woman, seeing that she could not prevail with her husband, spake to him again, saying, "If then I cannot prevail with thee that thou shouldest not put forth the child, yet listen to me. If the men must see a child put forth, do thou this thing that I shall tell thee. I was delivered of a child this day, and the child was dead when it was born. Take therefore this dead child and put it forth, and let us rear this child of the daughter of Astyages as if it were our own. So thou wilt not be found to transgress the commands of thy masters, and we shall also have done well for ourselves. For indeed the dead child shall have a royal burial, and the living child shall not be slain."

And here the woman seemed to her husband the herdsman to have spoken very wisely and seasonably, and he did according to her word. For the child that he had brought with him that he might cause him to die, this he gave to his wife to rear; and his own child, being dead already, he put into the basket wherein he had carried the other. With this he put all the ornaments wherewith the child had been adorned, and carried it to the most desolate place that he knew among the mountains, and there laid it forth. And on the third day after he had done this, he went again to the city, leaving his herds in the charge of one of them that were under him, and entering into the house of Harpagus, said he was ready to show the dead body of the child to any whom he might send. Wherefore Harpagus sent such of his own body-guard as he judged to be most faithful, and saw the thing, not himself indeed, but with their eyes, and afterwards buried the child that was the child of the herdsman. As for the child that had afterwards the name of Cyrus, the wife of the herdsman took him and reared him, but called him by some other name.

When the boy was ten years old there befell a thing by which his birth was discovered. He was wont to play with other boys that were his equals in age, in the village wherein were the dwellings of the herdsman and his fellows. And the boys in their sport chose him, being, as was supposed, the herdsman's son, to be their king. And he, being thus chosen, gave to each his proper work, setting one to build houses, and others to be his body-guards, and one to be the "Eye of the King," and others to carry messages, to each his own work. Now one of the boys that played with him, being the son of one Artembares, a man of renown among the Medes, would not do the thing which Cyrus had commanded him. Wherefore Cyrus bade the other boys lay hold of him; and when these had done his bidding he corrected him for his fault with many and grievous stripes. But the boy, so soon as he was let go, thinking that he had suffered a grievous wrong, went in great wrath to the city and made complaint to his father of the things which he had suffered at the hands of Cyrus; only he spake not of Cyrus, for he bare not as yet that name, but of the herdsman's son. Then Artembares, being in a great rage, went straightway to King Astyages, taking with him his son, as one that had been shamefully entreated.

And he said to the King, "See, O King, how we have been wronged by this slave who is the son of thy herdsman." And he showed him the lad's shoulders, where might be seen the marks of the stripes.

When Astyages heard and saw these things he was ready to avenge the lad on him that had done these things, wishing to do honour to Artembares. Therefore he sent for the herdsman and the boy. And when they were both come before him, Astyages looked towards Cyrus, "How didst thou, being the son of this herdsman, dare to do such shameful things to the son of a man who is first of all them that stand before me?"

To this Cyrus made answer, "My lord, all this

that I did, I did with good cause; for the boys of the village, this also being one of them, in their play chose me to be their king, for I seemed to them to be the fittest for this honour. All the others indeed did the things which I commanded them; but this boy was disobedient and paid no heed to me; for which things he received punishment as was due. And if thou deemest it fit that I should suffer for so doing, lo, here I am!"

When the lad spake in this fashion, Astyages, considering with himself the whole matter, knew him who he was. For the likeness of his countenance betrayed him; his speech also was more free than could be looked for in the son of a herdsman, and his age also agreed with the time of putting forth the child of his daughter. And being beyond measure astonished at these things, for a while he sat speechless; but at last, having scarcely come to himself, he said to Artembares, "Artembares, I will so deal with this matter that neither thou nor thy son shall blame me," for he would have the man go forth from his presence, that having the herdsman alone he might question him more closely concerning these matters.

Then the King sent Artembares away, and bade his servants take Cyrus with them into the house. Being therefore left alone with the herdsman, he enquired of him, saying, "Tell me whence didst thou receive this child, and who is he that gave him to thee?"

Then said the herdsman, "Surely he is my son, and she that bare him is my wife, and is yet alive in my house."

But the King answered, "Thou answerest not well for thyself; thou wilt bring thyself into great peril." And he bade his guards lay hold upon him. But the man, when he saw that he was being led away to the tormentors, said that he would tell the whole truth. And indeed he unfolded the story from the beginning, and neither changed nor concealed anything. And when he had ended, he was earnest in prayer to the King that he would have mercy upon him and pardon him.

As for the herdsman indeed, when he had thus told the truth, Astyages took little heed of him; but he had great wrath against Harpagus, and sent to him by his guards that he should come forthwith. And when he was come, the King said to him, "Harpagus, how didst thou slay the boy whom I delivered to thee that was born of my daughter?"

And Harpagus, seeing that the herdsman stood before the King, sought not to hide the matter, for he judged that he should be easily convicted if he should speak that which was false. Therefore he said, "O King, when I took the child from thy hands, I considered with myself how I might best do thy pleasure, so that I might both be blameless before thee, and also free of blood-guiltiness as concerning thy daughter. And I did after this manner. I called this herdsman to me, and gave the child into his hands, telling him that thou hadst given commandment that it should be slain. Then I bade him take the child, and put it out in some desert place among the mountains, and watch by it till it should die. And at the same time I used to him all manner of threats, if he should not in all things fulfill my words. And when the man had done according to my bidding, I sent the most faithful of my servants, and having seen by their eyes that the child was dead, I buried him. This is the truth of the matter, O King, and in this manner the child died."

When Harpagus had ended this story, wherein he spake, as he thought, the whole truth, Astyages hid his anger in his heart, and related the whole matter as he had heard it from the herdsman; and when it was ended, he said, "The boy yet lives; and it is well; for indeed I have been much troubled, remembering what had been done to the child; nor did I count it a light matter that my daughter was displeased with me. Now, therefore, that the matter hath turned out so well, first send thine own son that he may be a companion to this boy, and next come and dine with me to-day, for I would have a feast of thanksgiving for this boy that was dead and is alive again."

When Harpagus heard these words, he

bowed himself down before the King, rejoicing beyond measure that his transgression had had so good an ending, and that he had been called to the feast of thanksgiving; and he went to his house. And being come, in the joy of his heart he told to his wife all that had befallen him.

But the King, so soon as the son of Harpagus was come into the house, took him and slew him, and cut him limb from limb; and of the flesh he roasted some, and some he boiled; and so, having dressed it with much care, made it ready against the dinner. And when the hour of dinner was come, Harpagus and the other guests sat down to meat; and before Harpagus was set a dish of the flesh of his own son, wherein was every part, save only the head and the tips of the hands and of the feet. For these lay apart by themselves with a covering over them.

And when Harpagus had eaten enough, the King asked him, "Was this dish to thy mind." And when the man answered that it was indeed to his mind, certain men who had had commandment to do this thing brought the head and the hands and the feet, covered with their cover. These stood before Harpagus, and bade him uncover and take what he would. And when Harpagus so did, he saw what remained of his son. Yet, seeing it, he was not amazed, but still commanded himself. Then the King enquired of him, "Knowest thou what beast this is, of whom thou hast eaten?"

> And Harpagus made answer, "I know it; and all that the King doeth is well." Then he took what was left of the flesh and carried it with him to his house, and buried it."[9]

Astyages was more lenient with Cyrus, and allowed him to return to his biological parents, Cambyses and Mandané. Cyrus would grow up in the Median Empire, with his father, Cambyses, the king of Anshan.

Nebuchadnezzar's Successors

While Cyrus is growing up in Anshan, all the nations of the southern Levant region were serving Nebuchadnezzar. In 562 BC, Nebuchadnezzar died and was succeeded by his son Amel-Marduk, born of Nitocris, Princess of Egypt and Daughter of Necho II.[10] There was a marriage between Nebuchadneszzar and Nitocris that followed the Egyptians defeat at Carchemish, to form an alliance between the two nations. The reign of Amel-Marduk was from 562 BC to 560 BC.[11]

> In the thirty-seventh year of the exile of Jehoiachin king of Judah, in the year Evil-Merodach became king of Babylon, he released Jehoiachin king of Judah and freed him from prison ...
>
> Jeremiah 52:31 (NIV)

This is also mentioned in another part of the Bible, which may confirm that the author of 2 Kings wrote from the information gathered from other writers.

> In the thirty-seventh year of the exile of Jehoiachin king of Judah, in the year Evil-Merodach

became king of Babylon, he released Jehoiachin from prison ...

2 Kings 25:27 (NIV)

The Bible does not mention the other kings of Babylon; however, it is important to fill in the gaps to understand how the Living God moves through history.

Amel-Marduk was murdered by his brother-in-law, Nergal-Sharezer, more commonly referred to as Neriglissar, who then succeeded to the throne of Babylon in 560 BC. Neriglissar was married to Kashashaya, the daughter of Nebuchadnezzar and Nitocris. It was Neriglissar who released Jeremiah from prison back when Nebuchadnezzar invaded Jerusalem.

Now Nebuchadnezzar king of Babylon had given these orders about Jeremiah through Nebuzaradan commander of the imperial guard: "Take him and look after him; don't harm him but do for him whatever he asks." So Nebuzaradan the commander of the guard, Nebushazban a chief officer, *Nergal-Sharezer* a high official and all the other officers of the king of Babylon sent and had Jeremiah taken out of the courtyard of the guard. They turned him over to Gedaliah son of Ahikam, the son of Shaphan, to take him back to his home. So he remained among his own people.

Jeremiah 39:11–14 (NIV)

A year after Neriglissar took the throne in Babylon, 559 BC, Cyrus became the king of Anshan in the territory of the Median Empire after his father's death. Like his father, he recognized his grandfather, Astyages, as the king of Mede and his overlord. The rise of Cyrus as king will be important to the Israelites in Babylon, as they watch the soap opera of the Babylonian kings unfold.

In Babylon, it was in the third year (557/556 BC) of his reign that Neriglissar gathered his army and marched to Cilicia, to the north, to oppose Appuasu, the king of Pirindu, who had set out to plunder and sack Syria (Cilicia had two main cities on the plains. One of which was the residence of Paul, Tarsus). Before his arrival, Appuasu placed his army and cavalry, which he had organized, in a mountain valley and prepared to ambush the Babylonian army. The ambush failed, and when Neriglissar reached them he defeated Appuasu's army. Appuasu fled, but was pursued by Neriglissar as far as Ura, the royal city. He captured him, seized Ura, and sacked it. He then marched from Ura to Kirsi, his forefather's royal city, and captured it. He burnt its wall, its palace, and its people. Appuasu escaped; however, Neriglissar did not pursue him. He instead returned to Babylon.[12]

Following the death of Neriglissar in 556 BC, his son Labashi-Marduk (Nebuchadnezzar's grandson) became king of Babylon while still just a young boy. He was murdered a few months after his inauguration. Nabonidus, who was married to Niticris,[13] daughter of Nebuchadnezzar, was consequently chosen as the new king of Babylon, although Nabonidus was Assyrian and not Chaldean. Nabonidus allowed the religious practices of the Babylonian people to continue, while he himself worshiped the moon god "Sin" above all other gods. He paid special devotion to Sin's temple in Harran, where his mother was a priestess. By 553 BC, Nabonidus had moved to Tayma, a large oasis with a long history of settlement, located in northeastern Saudi Arabia at the point where the trade route begins to cross the Nefud desert. Nabonidus turned over the royal duties to his eldest son Belshazzar, making him a co-regent. Although Belshazzar is never king of Babylon, as co-regent he has the authority of king in his father's absence. During these years, idol worship and foreign gods are present in Babylon and the Babylonian Empire as well as the worship of the Living God of the Jews.

The Rise of Cyrus and the Persian Empire

In the Median Empire (554 BC), Cyrus King of Anshan rebelled against Mede due to his dissatisfaction with the policies of king Astyages, his grandfather. The revolt would last until 549 BC when Cyrus led his armies against the Medes and captured Ecbatana. Nabonidus tells us the story of Ecbatana in his chronicles. He says:

> King Astyages [litt: Ištumegu] called up his troops and marched against Cyrus [Kuraš], king of Anšan, in order to meet him in battle. The army of Astyages revolted against him and in fetters they delivered him to Cyrus. Cyrus marched against the country Agamtanu *[the Median capital Ecbatana]*; the royal residence he seized; silver, gold, other valuables of the country Agamtanu he took as booty and brought to Anšan.[14]

This defeat effectively conquered the Median Empire, and Cyrus would claim the royal crown of Mede. By 546

BC, he officially assumed the title of "king of Persia," as his father was Persian. Arsames, who had been the ruler of Persia under the Medes, therefore had to give up his throne, but would live to see his grandson become Darius the Great, the future King of Persia, after the deaths of both of Cyrus' sons. The defeat of Mede was only the start of things to come. Astyages had been allied with Croesus king of Lydia and Nabonidus king of Babylon. The three were in-laws by way of two marriages. The sister of Croesus was married to Astyages, and the sister of Astyages was married to Nebuchadnezzar, Nabopolassar's son. The alliance between these three Empires was strong, and they did not take kindly to what Cyrus had done.

The Lydian Empire included a number of Ionian Greek city-states of western Asia Minor, and allied itself with the Greek state of Sparta. Its capital city was Sardis. One of the most famous cities in Lydia was Troy. Croesus made war upon all the Greeks that dwelt in the western parts of Asia, looking for some reason to quarrel with every city. It did not matter what the reason, big or small; he would gladly use it to start something. Croesus subdued all the cities of the Greeks that were on the mainland of Lydia. Now the kingdom of Lydia flourished with great wealth and honor and all the wise men of the Greeks, as many as there were in those days, came to Sardis. Of those that came was Aesop, the author most commonly remembered for the fable "The Boy that Cried Wolf," but the greatest of all that came was Solon of Athens. Solon had created the laws for the Athenians, but then traveled for ten years as the Athenians were bound to live by them for that period of time. Croesus had great respect for Solon as a wise man and traveler.

{ On the third or fourth day after his coming the King commanded his servants that they should show Solon all the royal treasures. So the servants showed him all the things that the King possessed, a very great store of riches. And when he had seen everything and considered it, and a fitting time was come, the King said to him, "Man of Athens, I have heard much of thee in time past, of thy wisdom and of thy journeyings to and fro, for they say that thou wanderest over many lands, seeking for knowledge. I have therefore a desire to ask of thee one question: 'Whom thinkest thou to be the happiest of all men that thou hast seen?'"

And this he said hoping that Solon would answer, "Thou, O King, art the happiest man that I have seen."

But Solon flattered him not a whit, but spake the truth, saying, "O King, the happiest man that I have seen was Tellus the Athenian."

Then Crœsus, marveling much at these words, said, "And why thinkest thou that Tellus the Athenian was the happiest of men?"

Then Solon answered, "Tellus saw his country in great prosperity, and he had children born to him that were fair and noble, and to each of these also he saw children born, of whom there died not one. Thus did all things prosper with him in life, as we count prosperity, and the end of his days also was great and glorious; for when the Athenians fought with certain neighbors of theirs in Eleusis, he came to the help of his countrymen against their enemies, and put these to flight, and so died with great honour; and the whole people of the Athenians buried him in the same place wherein he fell, and honoured him greatly."

But when Solon had ended speaking to the King of Tellus, how happy he was, the King asked him again, "Whom, then, hast thou seen that is next in happiness to this Tellus?" For he thought to himself, "Surely now he will give me the second place."

Then Solon said, "I judge Cleobis and Biton to have been second in happiness to Tellus."

Cleobis and Biton were youths of the city of Argos. They had a livelihood such as sufficed them; and their strength was greater than that of other men. Not only did they win prizes of strength, but also they did this thing that shall now be told. The men of Argos held a feast to Here, who hath a great and famous temple in their city; and it must needs be that the mother of the two young men, being priestess of Here, should be drawn in a wagon from the city to the temple; but the oxen that should have drawn the wagon were not yet come from the fields. Then, as the time pressed and the matter was urgent, the young men harnessed themselves to the wagon and dragged it, and their mother the priestess sat upon it. And the space for which they dragged it was forty and five furlongs; and so they came to the temple. And when they had done this in the eyes of all the assembly, there befell them such a death that nothing could be more to be desired; the gods, indeed, making it manifest that it is far better for a man to die than to live. For indeed the thing fell out thus. When all the people of Argos came about the woman and her sons, and the men praised the youths for their great strength, and the women praised the mother that she had borne such noble sons, the mother in the joy of her heart stood before the image and prayed that the goddess would give to her sons, even Cleobis and Biton, that which the gods judge it best for a man to have. And when the priestess had so prayed, and the young men had offered sacrifice, and made merry with their companions, they lay down to sleep in the temple, and woke not again, but so ended their days. And the men of Argos commanded the artificers that they should make statues of the young men, and these they offered to the god at Delphi.

But when Solon thus gave the second place of happiness to these young men, King Crœsus was very wroth, and said, "Man of Athens, thou countest my happiness as nothing worth, not deeming me fit to be compared even with common men."

Then Solon made answer, "O Croesus, thou askest me about mortal life to say whether it be happy or no, but I know that the gods are jealous and apt to bring trouble upon men. I know also that if a man's years be prolonged he shall see many things that he would fain not see, aye, and suffer many things also. Now I reckon that the years of a man's life are threescore and ten, and that in these years there are twenty and five thousand days and two hundred. For this is the number, if a man reckon not the intercalated month. But if he reckon this, seeing that in threescore and ten years are thirty and five such months, and the days of these months are on thousand and fifty, then the whole sum of the days of a man's life is twenty and six thousand two hundred and fifty. Now of these days, being so many, not one bringeth to a man things like to those which another hath brought. Wherefore, O King, the whole life of a man is full of chance. I see indeed that thou hast exceeding great wealth and art king of many men. But as to that which thou askest of me, I call thee not happy, till I shall know that thou hast ended thy days prosperously. For the man that hath exceeding great riches is in no wise happier than he that hath sufficient only for the day, unless good fortune also remain with him, and give him all things that are to be desired, even unto the end of his days. For many men that are wealthy beyond measure are nevertheless unhappy, and many that have neither poverty nor riches have yet great happiness, and he that is exceeding rich and unhappy withal, excelleth him that hath moderate possessions with happiness in two things only, but the other excelleth in many things. For the first hath the more strength to satisfy the desires of his soul, and also to bear up against any misfortune that cometh upon him; but the second hath not this strength; and indeed he needeth it not, for his good fortune keepeth such things far from him. Also he is whole in body, and of good health, neither doth misfortune trouble him, and he hath good children, and is fair to look upon. And if, over and above these things, he also end his life well, then I judge him to be the happy man who thou seekest. But till he dies, so long do I hold my judgment, and call him not happy indeed, but fortunate. It is impossible also that any man should comprehend in his life all things that be good. For even as a country sufficeth not for itself nor produceth all things, but hath certain things of its own and receiveth certain from others, and as that country which produceth the most is counted the best, even so is it with men, for no man's body sufficeth for all things, but hath one thing and lacketh another. Whosoever, O King, keepeth ever the greatest store of things, and so endeth his life in a seemly fashion, this man deserveth in my judgment to be called happy. But we must needs regard the end of all things, how they shall turn out; for the gods give to many men some earnest of happiness, but yet in the end overthrow them utterly."

These were the words of Solon. But they pleased not King Croesus by any means. Therefore the King made no account of him, and dismissed him as being a foolish and ignorant person, seeing that he took no heed of the blessings that men have in their hands, bidding them always have regard unto their end.[15]

Around 547 BC, King Croesus of Lydia decided that it was a good time to attack the Median state and seek revenge for his brother-in-law Astyages. Croesus figured that Cyrus' army would be disorganized after his battles with the Medes. However, prior to invading the city of Pteria in Cappadocia, Croesus asked the Oracle of Delphi what would happen if he attacked Cyrus' army. He was told by the Pythia, "If Croesus make war against the Persians, he shall bring to the ground a great empire."[16] Croesus did not realize that it would be his kingdom to fall and not Cyrus.'

Cyrus captured Croesus in Sardis and placed him on a large "pyre," a wooden pile used to burn a body as part of a funeral rite. Cyrus wanted to see if any heavenly powers would appear to save him from being burned alive. The pyre was set on fire and Cyrus heard Croesus call out "Solon!," the meaning of which was told to Cyrus that Solon had warned Croesus of the fickleness of good fortune. That one should consider the end of life, and not boast on slippery grounds of foolish prosperity, since no man is happy until he has died well. Cyrus ordered the fire to be put out, because he realized Croesus was a lot like himself. Cyrus was convinced that Croesus was a good man, so he made Croesus an advisor in his court.[17] By 542 BC, Cyrus had incorporated the Lydian Empire and Cilicia into the Persian Empire and turned his attention to the Babylonian Empire and Nabonidus, the ally of Croesus.

Cyrus believed that he was the chosen ruler of a supreme deity, although he believed it to be the Babylonian god Marduk, not the God of Israel. He had not acknowledged the God of Israel, but this was prophesied by Isaiah in 712 BC when he said:

> "This is what the LORD says to his anointed, to Cyrus, whose right hand I take hold of to subdue nations before him and to strip kings of their armor, to open doors before him so that gates will not be shut: I will go before you and will level the mountains; I will break down gates of bronze and cut through bars of iron. I will give you the treasures of darkness, riches stored in secret places, so that you may know that I am the LORD, the God of Israel, who summons you by name. For the sake of Jacob my servant, of Israel my chosen, I summons you by name and bestow on you a title of honor, though you do not acknowledge me. I am the LORD, and there is no other; apart from me there is no God. I will strengthen you,

> though you have not acknowledged me so that
> from the rising of the sun to the place of its
> setting men may know there is none besides me.
> I am the LORD, and there is no other. I form the
> light and create darkness, I bring prosperity and
> create disaster; I, the LORD, do all these things."
>
> Isaiah 45:1–5 (NIV)

An interesting parallel can be drawn between Cyrus and Jesus. Their births were both prophesied, both were threats to the king, both were in danger to be murdered after their birth, and they both were destined to redeem the Jews. The lives of Nebuchadnezzar and Cyrus show that the Living God, the God of Abraham will use anyone he chooses to fulfill his commands. If His people do not worship Him, but instead fall into sorcery and pagan worship, he will send foreign nations in to destroy them:

> "Yet even in those days,' declares the LORD, 'I
> will not destroy you completely. And when the
> people ask, 'Why has the LORD our God done
> all this to us?' you will tell them, 'As you have
> forsaken me and served foreign gods in your own
> land, so now you will serve foreigners in a land
> not your own.'"
>
> Jeremiah 5:15–19

Fall of Babylon

Now Nabonidus had returned to Babylon around 540 BC because Cyrus was about to invade. In 539 BC, Nabonidus gathered all of the most important cultic statues from all over southern Mesopotamia in Babylon, just before the Persian attack. This was not a sign of blasphemy of some sort, but part of his defense of Babylonia: by gathering the statues, Nabonidus tried to ensure the support of the gods in the upcoming war against the Persians:

> "In the month of [Âbu?] Lugal-Marada and the other gods of the town Marad, Zabada and the other gods of Kish, the goddess Ninlil and the other gods of Hursagkalama visited Babylon. Till the end of the month Ulûlu all the gods of Akkad–those from above and those from below– entered Babylon. The gods of Borsippa, Cutha, and Sippar did not enter."[18]
>
> Babylonian Chronicles on the seventeenth year of Nabonidus

In 539 BC, Cyrus' armies, under the command of Gubaru, the governor of Gutium, attacked Opis on the Tigris river and were met by Nabonidus and the Babylonian army. In the ensuing battle, the Persians booked a minor victory, not sufficient for Nabonidus to be defeated altogether, but enough for the Persians to be able to massacre the people of Opis, which in turn caused the nearby city of Sippar to surrender. Cyrus sent a small division south to try and take the capital, Babylon, by surprise. Herodotus explains that to accomplish this feat, the Persians diverted the Euphrates River into a canal so that the water level dropped "to the height of the middle of a man's thigh," which allowed the invading forces to march directly through the river bed to enter at night. This plan worked and the city was taken without a battle. Not knowing that the capital had been taken by Cyrus, Nabonidus returned to Babylon from his armies near the Euphrates and was captured. About seventeen days later, Cyrus himself entered the city of Babylon and arrested Nabonidus. He then assumed the titles of "king of Babylon, king of Sumer and Akkad, king of the four sides of the world."[18]

On the night that the Persian army was invading Babylon, Belshazzar was having a banquet, unaware that Cyrus had sent troops to the city. During the banquet, he brought in the gold and silver goblets that Nebuchadnezzar had taken from the temple of Jerusalem so that the king, his nobles, his wives and his concubines might drink from them. As they were drinking, there suddenly appeared a finger of a human hand, writing on the wall. Belshazzar ordered the writing to be interpreted, but none could do so. It was Daniel, the exile from Judah, now probably in his 70s, that interpreted the writing. This is what Daniel said:

O king, the Most High God gave your (grand) father Nebuchadnezzar sovereignty and greatness and glory and splendor. Because of the high position he gave him, all the peoples and nations and men of every language dreaded and feared him. Those the king wanted to put to death, he put to death; those he wanted to spare, he spared; those he wanted to promote, he promoted; and those he wanted to humble, he humbled. But when his heart became arrogant and hardened with pride, he was deposed from his royal throne and stripped of his glory. He was driven away from people and given the mind of an animal; he lived with the wild donkeys and ate grass like cattle; and his body was drenched with the dew of heaven, until he acknowledged that the Most High God is sovereign over the kingdoms of men and sets over them anyone he wishes.

But you his (grand) son, O Belshazzar, have not humbled yourself, though you knew all this. Instead, you have set yourself up against the Lord of heaven. You had the goblets from his temple brought to you, and you and your nobles, your wives and your concubines drank wine from them. You praised the gods of silver and gold, of bronze, iron, wood and stone, which cannot see or hear or understand. But you did not honor the God who holds in his hand your life and all your ways. Therefore he sent the hand that wrote the inscription.

> This is the inscription that was written:
> Mene, Mene, Tekel, Parsin
> This is what these words mean:
> Mene: God has numbered the days of your reign and brought it to an end.
> Tekel: You have been weighed on the scales and found wanting.
> Peres [the singular to Parsin]: Your kingdom is divided and given to the Medes and Persians."
> Then at Belshazzar's command, Daniel was clothed in purple, a gold chain was placed around his neck, and he was proclaimed the third highest ruler in the kingdom.
>
> Daniel 5:18–29 (NIV)

If Belshazzar (the co-regent) were the king, then Daniel would have been made the second highest ruler in the kingdom. But because Belshazzar's father, Nabonidus was still alive and still the king, there were already two rulers in the kingdom. So Daniel was made the third ruler. This was all for nothing anyway, since that very night Cyrus' army had entered the city and had taken control.

Jeremiah had prophesied that: "…All nations will serve him [Nebuchadnezzar] and his son and his grandson until the time for his land comes; then many nations and great kings will subjugate him." (Jeremiah 27:7, NIV)

The grandson of Nebuchadnezzar, both Labashi-Marduk and now Belshazzar (as the co-regent), has served as king. The time for his land had come! (538 BC)

Before leaving Babylon, Cyrus issued that the gods which Nabonidus had brought to Babylon be returned to their sacred cities:[18]

> ... at the command of Marduk, the great LORD, I settled in their habitations, in pleasing abodes, the gods of Sumer and Akkad, whom Nabonidus, to the anger of the LORD of the gods, had brought into Babylon.
>
> May all the gods whom I settled in their sacred centers ask daily of Bêl and Nâbu that my days be long and may they intercede for my welfare. May they say to Marduk, my lord: "As for Cyrus, the king who reveres you, and Cambyses, his son."[19]
>
> The Cyrus Cylinder, lines 30–36

The God of Judah had no temple to be returned to, because Nebuchadnezzar had destroyed it. To please the God of Judah, Cyrus issued the "Edict of Restoration," for it had been prophesied by the prophet Isaiah one hundred years before the destruction of Jerusalem that Cyrus would be their redeemer and would instruct the Jewish people to rebuild the temple. "... who says of Cyrus, 'He is my shepherd and will accomplish all that I please; he will say of Jerusalem, "Let it be rebuilt," and of the temple, "Let its foundations be laid" (Isaiah 44:28, NIV). Cyrus was not acknowledging the Living God, the God of the Jews, as his god. He was attempting to appease all the gods by returning them to their sacred places, since they did not prevent him from conquering the Babylonian Empire. He believed that by returning all the gods to their temples, the gods would honor him and his kingdom.

This is what was prophesied by Isaiah:

> "For the sake of Jacob my servant, of Israel my chosen, I summons you by name and bestow on you a title of honor, though you do not acknowledge me. I am the LORD, and there is no other; apart from me there is no God. I will strengthen you, though you have not acknowledged me…"
>
> Isaiah 45:4–5 (NIV)

The Jews proclaimed Cyrus as their redeemer, and they gave the name of Cyrus honor. Because of their redemption, the Jews return to worshiping God in the ways of their ancestors.

Because of the Assyrian deportation and the Babylonian exile of the Jews, there were Jews throughout the newly formed Persian Empire, and a renewed worship of the Living God through Judaism. Cyrus authorized the rebuilding of the temple to the God of heaven, and gave all of the Jews that wished to leave permission to return to Jerusalem. Not all of them would leave. Many had married and had families, as was instructed by Jeremiah. They stayed in the Babylonian area now controlled by the Persians, and would spread throughout the Persian Empire. Cyrus was open to all forms of religious worship and did not prevent anyone from worshiping as they pleased.

Cyrus leaves the governing of Babylon to Gobryas, his governor. Gobryas installs sub-governors to rule Babylon:

> In the month of Arahsamna, the third day [29 October], Cyrus entered Babylon, [unidentified objects] were filled before him - the state of peace was imposed upon the city. Cyrus sent greetings to all Babylon. Gobryas, his governor, installed sub-governors in Babylon.
>
> From the month of Kislîmu to the month of Addaru, the gods of Akkad which Nabonidus had made come down to Babylon, were returned to their sacred cities.
>
> In the month of Arahsamna, on the night of the eleventh, Gobryas died [6 November].[18]

The Book of Daniel says that:

> It pleased Darius to appoint 120 satraps to rule throughout the kingdom, with three administrators over them, one of whom was Daniel. The satraps were made accountable to them so that the king might not suffer loss. Now Daniel so distinguished himself among the administrators and the satraps by his exceptional qualities that the king planned to set him over the whole kingdom.
>
> Daniel 6:1-3 (NIV)

During that same year, Cyrus incorporates Susiana into the Persian Empire and the new empire looked something like the following figure.

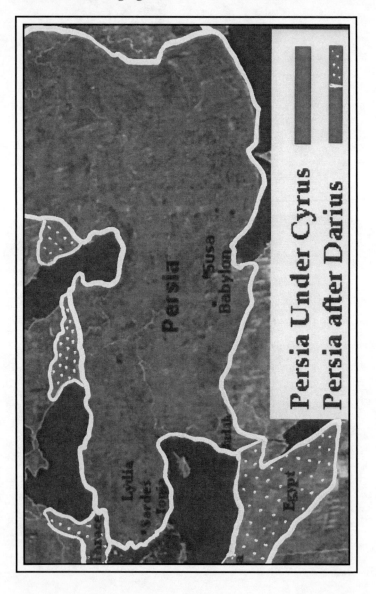

It is believed that Gobryas is the "Darius" mentioned in this passage, because Darius appoints satraps (governors) to rule in Babylon. According to the Cyrus cylinder, Gobryas rules for one year and dies. The book of Daniel only mentions the "first year of Darius' reign". It never talks about a second year, so it is plausible that this is the correct interpretation. It is during this year that Daniel is thrown in the lions den and comes out unharmed. Gobryas issues a decree:

> "I issue a decree that in every part of my kingdom people must fear and reverence the God of Daniel. For he is the living God and he endures forever; his kingdom will not be destroyed, his dominion will never end. He rescues and he saves; he performs signs and wonders in the heavens and on the earth. He has rescued Daniel from the power of the lions."
>
> So Daniel prospered during the reign of Darius and the reign of Cyrus [a] the Persian.
>
> Daniel 6:26-28 (NIV)

With this decree, the worship and praise of God can continue in the new Persian Empire.

The rebuilding of the temple in Jerusalem did not proceed without conflict. When the Samaritans had heard that the exiles were rebuilding the temple for the Lord, the God of Israel, they insisted on helping with the construction; after all, they too worshiped the same God and had been sacrificing to Him since they were brought to Samaria by the king of Assyria. But Judah considered the Samaritans as "not of their people" and not worthy to build the Lord's temple, and sent them away. This did not sit well with the Samaritans and they petitioned the king of Persia to stop the construction.[20] This would become the source of the feud between the Jews and the Samaritans that would last even after Jesus' days, as told in the parable of the "Good Samaritan."

Upon the death of Cyrus, king of Persia in 530 BC, Cambyses II, Cyrus' son, became king of Persia. Cambyses moved the Persian capital from Pasagadae to Susa. According to Josephus, it was Cambyses that was convinced to stop the rebuilding of the temple and the city of Jerusalem because he was told that the Jews were rebellious and wicked and that the Jews would not pay tribute or submit to his commands once the walls were up. Cambyses had his scribes search the books of his forefathers and found that the Jewish people did have a history of being enemies to kings and raising seditions and wars. He therefore ordered the re-building efforts halted.[21]

Cambyses began to look toward Egypt. His anger was stirred by the events as told by the historian Herodotus.

> The reason of the invasion was the following. Cambyses, by the advice of a certain Egyptian, who was angry with Amasis for having torn him from his wife and children and given him over to the Persians, had sent a herald to Amasis to

ask his daughter in marriage. His adviser was a physician, whom Amasis, when Cyrus had requested that he would send him the most skilful of all the Egyptian eye-doctors, singled out as the best from the whole number. Therefore the Egyptian bore Amasis a grudge, and his reason for urging Cambyses to ask the hand of the king's daughter was, that if he complied, it might cause him annoyance; if he refused, it might make Cambyses his enemy. When the message came, Amasis, who much dreaded the power of the Persians, was greatly perplexed whether to give his daughter or no; for that Cambyses did not intend to make her his wife, but would only receive her as his concubine, he knew for certain. He therefore cast the matter in his mind, and finally resolved what he would do. There was a daughter of the late king Apries, named Nitetis, a tall and beautiful woman, the last survivor of that royal house. Amasis took this woman, and decking her out with gold and costly garments, sent her to Persia as if she had been his own child. Some time afterwards, Cambyses, as he gave her an embrace, happened to call her by her father's name, whereupon she said to him, "I see, O king, thou knowest not how thou has been cheated by Amasis; who took me, and, tricking me out with gauds, sent me to thee as his own daughter. But I am in truth the child of Apries, who was his lord and master, until he rebelled against him, together with the rest of the Egyptians, and put him to death."

It was this speech, and the cause of quarrel it disclosed, which roused the anger of Cambyses, son of Cyrus, and brought his arms upon Egypt.[22]

It was this woman that induced Cambyses to begin a war with Egypt, for the obvious reason of revenge for her father's death. Before Cambyses left on his Egyptian conquest, he had a dream that Smerdis would sit on his throne if he left. So before leaving he secretly had Smerdis, his brother, murdered in order to prevent Smerdis from rebelling during his absence. The conquest of Egypt was successful and Cambyses became king of Egypt.

Pythagoras

While in Egypt, Cambyses found a notable Greek who was there studying with the priests. His name was Pythagoras. Many know of Pythagoras from the mathematical calculations he is credited for having developed, particularly the Pythagorean Theorem: $a^2 + b^2 = c^2$. The purpose of Pythagoras' visit to Egypt stemmed from his birth.

[His father] Mnesarchus had gone to Delphi on a business trip, leaving his wife without any signs of pregnancy. He enquired of the oracle about the event of his return voyage to Syria, and he was informed that his trip would be lucrative, and most conformable to his wishes; but that his wife was now with child, and would present him with a son who would surpass all who had ever lived in beauty and wisdom, and that he would be of the greatest benefit to the human race in everything pertaining to human achievements. When Mnesarchus realized that the god, without waiting for any question about a son, had by an oracle informed him that he would possess an illustrious prerogative, and truly divine gift, he immediately changed his wife's former name Parthenis to one reminiscent of the Delphic prophet and her son, naming her Pythais, and the infant, who was soon after born at Sidon in Phoenicia, Pythagoras, by this name commemorating that such an offspring had been promised him by the Pythian Apollo.

The assertions of Epimenides, Eudoxus and Xenocrates, that Apollo having at that time already had actual connection with Parthenis, causing her pregnancy, had regularized that fact by predicting the birth of Pythagoras, are by no means to be admitted. No one will deny that the soul of Pythagoras was sent to mankind from Apollo's domain, having either been one of his attendants, or more intimate associates, which may be inferred both from his birth, and his versatile wisdom.

After Mnesarchus had returned from Syria to Samos, with great wealth derived from a favorable sea-voyage, he built a temple to Apollo, with the inscription of Pythius. He took care that his son should enjoy the best possible education, studying under Creophilus, then under Phorecydos the Syrian, and then under almost all who presided over sacred concerns, to who he especially recommended his son, that he might be as expert as possible in divinity. Thus by education and good fortune he became the most beautiful and godlike of all those who have been celebrated in the annals of history.

After his father's death, though he was still

but a youth, his aspect was so venerable, and his habits so temperate that he was honored and even reverenced by elderly men, attracting the attention of all who saw and heard him speak, creating the most profound impression. That is the reason that many plausibly asserted that he was a child of the divinity. Enjoying the privilege of such a renown, of an education so thorough from infancy, and of so impressive a natural appearance he showed that he deserved all these advantages by deserving them, by the adornment of piety and discipline, by exquisite habits, by firmness of soul, and by a body duly subjected to the mandates of reason. An inimitable quiet and serenity marked all his words and actions, soaring above all laughter, emulation, contention, or any other irregularity or eccentricity; his influence at Samos was that of some beneficent divinity. His great renown, while yet a youth, reached not only men as illustrious for their wisdom as Thales at Miletus, and Bias at Prione, but also extended to the neighboring cities. He was celebrated everywhere as the "long-haired Samian," and by the multitude was given credit for being under divine inspiration.

When he had attained his eighteenth year, there arose the tyranny of Policrates; and Pythagoras foresaw that under such a government his studies might be impeded, as they engrossed the whole of his attention. So by night he privately departed with one Hermodamas, - who was surnamed Creophilus, and was the grandson of the host, friend and general preceptor of the poet Homer, - going to Phorecydos, to Anaximander the natural philosopher, and to Thales at Miletu. He successively associated with each of those philosophers in a manner such that they all loved him, admired his natural endowments, and admitted him to the best of their doctrines, Thales especially, on gladly admitting him to the intimacies of his confidence, admired the great difference between him and other young men, who were in every accomplishment surpassed by Pythagoras. After increasing the reputation Pythagoras had already acquired, by communicating to him the utmost he was able to impart to him, Thales, laying stress on his advanced age and the infirmities of his body, advised him to go to Egypt, to get in touch with the priests of Memphis and Jupiter. Thales confessed that the instruction of these priests was the source of his own reputation for wisdom, while neither his own endowments nor achievements equaled those which were so evident in Pythagoras. Thales insisted that, in view of all this, if Pythagoras should study with those priests, he was certain of becoming the wisest and most divine of men.

Here in Egypt he frequented all the temples with the greatest diligence, and most studious research, during which time he won the esteem and admiration of all the priests and prophets with whom he associated. Having most solicitously familiarized himself with every detail, he did not, nevertheless, neglect any contemporary celebrity, whether sage renowned for wisdom, or peculiarly performed mystery; he did not fail to visit any place where he thought he might discover something worthwhile. That is how he visited all of the Egyptian priests, acquiring all the wisdom each possessed. He thus passed twenty-two years in the sanctuaries of temples, studying astronomy and geometry, and being initiated in no casual or superficial manner in all the mysteries of the gods. At length, however, he was taken captive by the soldiers of Cambyses, and carried off to Babylon. Here he was overjoyed to associate with the Magi, who instructed him in their venerable knowledge, and in the most perfect worship of the gods. Through their assistance, likewise, he studied and completed arithmetic, music, and all the other sciences. After twelve years, about the fifty-sixth year of his age, he returned to Samos.[23]

Pythagoras was one of the first to believe and proclaim that the earth was round, that all planets have an axis, and that all the planets travel around one central point. He originally identified that point as Earth, but later renounced it for the idea that the planets revolve around a central "fire" that he never identified as the sun. He also believed that the moon was another planet that he called a "counter-Earth."

While in exile, Daniel, the Jew, was appointed as the head of the wise men, the Chaldean Magi, after impressing King Nebuchadnezzar by interpreting his dreams. It is believed that Daniel did not live to see Cambyses become king since he is not mentioned in the Bible. His training of the Chaldean Magi, and his leadership did however live on. Pythagoras' association with the Magi, while in Babylon educated him on the worship of Judaism as well as math, astronomy, and the practice of cultic religions. He then brought that knowledge back to Samos and Greece and taught it to his students, the Pythagoreans. Pythagoras' twelve years in Babylon means that he also crossed paths with Zorobabel, Haggai, and Zechariah. Flavius Josephus writes:

> … But now it is proper to satisfy the inquiry of those that disbelieve the records of barbarians, and think none but Greeks to be worthy of credit, and to produce many of these very Greeks who were acquainted with our nation (Jewish Nation), and to set before them such as upon occasion have made mention of us in their own writings. Pythagoras, therefore, of Samos, lived in very ancient times, and was esteemed a person superior to all philosophers in wisdom and piety towards God. Now it is plain that he did not only know our doctrines, but was in very great

measure a follower and admirer of them. There is not indeed extant any writing that is owned for his but many there are who have written his history, of whom Hermippus is the most celebrated, who was a person very inquisitive into all sorts of history. Now this Hermippus, in his first book concerning Pythagoras, speaks thus: "That Pythagoras, upon the death of one of his associates, whose name was Calliphon, a Crotonlate by birth, affirmed that this man's soul conversed with him both night and day, and enjoined him not to pass over a place where an ass had fallen down; as also not to drink of such waters as caused thirst again; and to abstain from all sorts of reproaches." After which he adds thus: "This he did and said in imitation of the doctrines of the Jews and Thracians, which he transferred into his own philosophy." For it is very truly affirmed of this Pythagoras, that he took a great many of the laws of the Jews into his own philosophy.[24]

Pythagoras was born around 578 BC and died around 490 BC during the Ionian revolt, but not as a result of the revolt. It should not be taken that Pythagoras was a true follower of the Jewish practices, only that he incorporated some of their laws into his own philosophy, bringing that knowledge to the Greeks. The Chaldean Magi, judging from their various tenets, which included a divine triad, pantheism, magic, astrology, number mysticism, the belief in reincarnation and the four elements (water, fire, earth, and air), was closer in similarity to the Kabbalah. The Kabbalah is also believed to have originated in Babylon.

Darius

During the absence of Cambyses from Susa while in Egypt, an imposter, a Magian also named Smerdis, posed as his brother Smerdis and claimed the throne of Persia. Cambyses began to march against him but died in 522 BC, before reaching the imposter. Darius, along with six others, learned of the imposter. Herodotus tells the story as follows:

Thus then Cambyses died, and the Magus now reigned in security, and passed himself off for Smerdis the son of Cyrus. And so went by the seven months which were wanting to complete the eighth year of Cambyses. His subjects, while his reign lasted, received great benefits from him, insomuch that, when he died, all the dwellers in Asia mourned his loss exceedingly, except only the Persians. For no sooner did he come to the throne than forthwith he sent round to every nation under his rule, and granted them freedom from war-service and from taxes for the space of three years.

In the eighth month, however, it was discovered who he was in the mode following. There was a man called Otanes, the son of Pharnaspes, who for rank and wealth was equal to the greatest of the Persians. This Otanes was the first to suspect that the Magus was not Smerdis the son of Cyrus, and to surmise moreover who he really was. He was led to guess the truth by the king never quitting the citadel, and never calling before him any of the Persian noblemen. As soon, therefore, as his suspicions were aroused he adopted the following measures: One of his daughters, who was called Phaedima, had been married to Cambyses, and was taken to wife, together with the rest of Cambyses' wives, by the Magus. To this daughter Otanes sent a message, and inquired of her "who it was whose bed she shared,- was it Smerdis the son of Cyrus, or was it some other man?" Phaedima in reply declared she did not know- Smerdis the son of Cyrus she had never seen, and so she could not tell whose bed she shared. Upon this Otanes sent a second time, and said, "If thou dost not know Smerdis son of Cyrus thyself, ask queen Atossa who it is with whom ye both live- she cannot fail to know her own brother."

To this the daughter made answer, "I can neither get speech with Atossa, nor with any of the women who lodge in the palace. For no sooner did this man, be he who he may, obtain the kingdom, than he parted us from one another, and gave us all separate chambers."

This made the matter seem still more plain to Otanes. Nevertheless he sent a third message to his daughter in these words following: "Daughter, thou art of noble blood- thou wilt not shrink from a risk which thy father bids thee encounter. If this fellow be not Smerdis the son of Cyrus, but the man whom I think him to be, his boldness in taking thee to be his wife, and lording it over the Persians, must not be allowed to pass unpunished. Now therefore do as I command—when next he passes the night with thee, wait till thou art sure he is fast asleep, and then feel for his ears. If thou findest him to have ears, then believe him to be Smerdis the son of Cyrus, but if he has none, know him for Smerdis the Magian." Phaedima returned for answer, "It would be a great risk. If he was without ears, and caught her feeling for them, she well knew he would make away with her—nevertheless she would venture." So Otanes got his daughter's promise that she would do as he desired. Now Smerdis the Magian had had his ears cut off in the lifetime of Cyrus son of Cambyses, as a punishment for a crime of no slight heinousness. Phaedima therefore, Otanes' daughter, bent on accomplishing what she had promised her father, when her turn came, and she was taken to the bed of the Magus (in Persia a man's wives sleep with him in their turns), waited till he was sound asleep, and then felt for his ears. She quickly perceived that he had no ears; and of this, as soon as day dawned, she sent word to her father.

Then Otanes took to him two of the chief Persians, Aspathines and Gobryas, men whom it was most advisable to trust in such a matter, and told them everything. Now they had already of themselves suspected how the matter stood. When Otanes therefore laid his reasons before them they at once came into his views; and it was agreed that each of the three should take as companion in the work the Persian in whom he placed the greatest confidence. Then Otanes chose Intaphernes, Gobryas Megabyzus, and Aspathines Hydarnes. After the number had thus become six, Darius, the son of Hystaspes, arrived at Susa from Persia, whereof his father was governor. On his coming it seemed good to the six to take him likewise into their counsels.

After this, the men, being now seven in all, met together to exchange oaths, and hold discourse with one another. And when it came to the turn of Darius to speak his mind, he said as follows: "Methought no one but I knew that Smerdis, the son of Cyrus, was not now alive, and that Smerdis the Magian ruled over us; on this account I came hither with speed, to compass the death of the Magian. But as it seems the matter is known to you all, and not to me only, my judgment is that we should act at once, and not any longer delay. For to do so were not well."

Otanes spoke upon this: "Son of Hystaspes," said he, "thou art the child of a brave father, and seemest likely to show thyself as bold a gallant as he. Beware, however, of rash haste in this matter; do not hurry so, but proceed with soberness. We must add to our number ere we adventure to strike the blow."

"Not so," Darius rejoined; "for let all present be well assured that if the advice of Otanes guide our acts, we shall perish most miserably. Some one will betray our plot to the Magians for lucre's sake. Ye ought to have kept the matter to yourselves, and so made the venture; but as ye have chosen to take others into your secret, and have opened the matter to me, take my advice and make the attempt today- or if not, if a single day be suffered to pass by, be sure that I will let no one betray me to the Magian. I myself will go to him, and plainly denounce you all."

Otanes, when he saw Darius so hot, replied, "But if thou wilt force us to action, and not allow a day's delay, tell us, I pray thee, how we shall get entrance into the palace, so as to set upon them. Guards are placed everywhere, as thou thyself well knowest- for if thou hast not seen, at least thou hast heard tell of them. How are we to pass these guards, I ask thee?"

Answered Darius, "there are many things easy enough in act, which by speech it is hard to explain. There are also things concerning which speech is easy, but no noble action follows when the speech is done. As for these guards, ye know well that we shall not find it hard to make our way through them. Our rank alone would cause them to allow us to enter- shame and fear alike forbidding them to say us nay. But besides, I have the fairest plea that can be conceived for gaining admission. I can say that I have just come from Persia, and have a message to deliver to the king from my father. An untruth must be spoken, where need requires. For whether men lie, or say true, it is with one and the same object. Men lie, because they think to gain by deceiving others; and speak the truth, because they expect to get something by their true speaking, and to be trusted afterwards in more important matters. Thus, though their conduct is so opposite, the end of both is alike. If there were no gain to be got, your true-speaking man would tell untruths as much as your liar, and your liar would tell the truth as much as your true-speaking man. The doorkeeper, who lets us in readily, shall have his guerdon some day or other; but woe to the man who resists us, he must forthwith be declared an enemy. Forcing our way past him, we will press in and go straight to our work."

After Darius had thus said, Gobryas spoke as follows: "Dear friends, when will a fitter occasion offer for us to recover the kingdom, or, if we are not strong enough, at least die in the attempt? Consider that we Persians are governed by a Median Magus, and one, too, who has had his ears cut off! Some of you were present when Cambyses lay upon his deathbed- such, doubtless, remember what curses he called down upon the Persians if they made no effort to recover the kingdom. Then, indeed, we paid but little heed to what he said, because we thought he spoke out of hatred to set us against his brother. Now, however, my vote is that we do as Darius has counseled- march straight in a body to the palace from the place where we now are, and forthwith set upon the Magian." So Gobryas spake, and the others all approved.

While the seven were thus taking counsel together, it so chanced that the following events were happening: The Magi had been thinking what they had best do, and had resolved for many reasons to make a friend of Prexaspes. They knew how cruelly he had been outraged by Cambyses, who slew his son with an arrow; they were also aware that it was by his hand that Smerdis the son of Cyrus fell, and that he was the only person privy to that prince's death; and they further found him to be held in the highest esteem by all the Persians. So they called him to them, made him their friend, and bound him by a promise and by oaths to keep silence about the fraud which they were practicing upon the Persians, and not discover it to any one; and they pledged themselves that in this case they would give him thousands of gifts of every sort and kind. So Prexaspes agreed, and the Magi, when they found that they had persuaded him so far, went on to another proposal, and said they would assemble the Persians at the foot of the palace wall, and he should mount one of the towers and harangue them from it, assuring them that Smerdis the son of Cyrus, and none but he, ruled the land. This they bade him do, because Prexaspes was a man of great weight with his countrymen, and had often declared in public that Smerdis the son of Cyrus was still alive, and denied being his murderer.

Prexaspes said he was quite ready to do their will in the matter; so the Magi assembled the people, and placed Prexaspes upon the top of the tower, and told him to make his speech. Then this man, forgetting of set purpose all that the Magi had entreated him to say, began with Achaeamenes, and traced down the descent of Cyrus; after which, when he came to that king, he recounted all the services that had been rendered by him to the Persians, from whence he went on to declare the truth, which hitherto he had concealed, he said, because it would not have been safe for him to make it known, but now necessity was laid on him to disclose the whole. Then he told how, forced to it by Cambyses, he had himself taken the life of Smerdis, son of Cyrus, and how that Persia was now ruled by the Magi. Last of all, with many curses upon the

Persians if they did not recover the kingdom, and wreak vengeance on the Magi, he threw himself headlong from the tower into the abyss below. Such was the end of Prexaspes, a man all his life of high repute among the Persians.

And now the seven Persians, having resolved that they would attack the Magi without more delay, first offered prayers to the gods and then set off for the palace, quite unacquainted with what had been done by Prexaspes. The news of his doings reached them upon their way, when they had accomplished about half the distance. Hereupon they turned aside out of the road, and consulted together. Otanes and his party said they must certainly put off the business, and not make the attack when affairs were in such a ferment. Darius, on the other hand, and his friends, were against any change of plan, and wished to go straight on, and not lose a moment. Now, as they strove together, suddenly there came in sight two pairs of vultures, and seven pairs of hawks, pursuing them, and the hawks tore the vultures both with their claws and bills. At this sight the seven with one accord came in to the opinion of Darius, and encouraged by the omen hastened on towards the palace.

At the gate they were received as Darius had foretold. The guards, who had no suspicion that they came for any ill purpose, and held the chief Persians in much reverence, let them pass without difficulty- it seemed as if they were under the special protection of the gods- none even asked them any question. When they were now in the great court they fell in with certain of the eunuchs, whose business it was to carry the king's messages, who stopped them and asked what they wanted, while at the same time they threatened the doorkeepers for having let them enter. The seven sought to press on, but the eunuchs would not suffer them. Then these men, with cheers encouraging one another, drew their daggers, and stabbing those who strove to withstand them, rushed forward to the apartment of the males.

Now both the Magi were at this time within, holding counsel upon the matter of Prexaspes. So when they heard the stir among the eunuchs, and their loud cries, they ran out themselves, to see what was happening. Instantly perceiving their danger, they both flew to arms; one had just time to seize his bow, the other got hold of his lance; when straightway the fight began. The one whose weapon was the bow found it of no service at all; the foe was too near, and the combat too close to allow of his using it. But the other made a stout defense with his lance, wounding two of the seven, Aspathines in the leg, and Intaphernes in the eye. This wound did not kill Intaphernes, but it cost him the sight of that eye. The other Magus, when he found his bow of no avail, fled into a chamber which opened out into the apartment of the males, intending to shut to the doors. But two of the seven entered the room with him, Darius and Gobryas. Gobryas seized the Magus and grappled with him, while Darius stood over them, not knowing what to do; for it was dark, and he was afraid that if he struck a blow he might kill Gobryas.

Then Gobryas, when he perceived that Darius stood doing nothing, asked him, "why his hand was idle?"

"I fear to hurt thee," he answered.

"Fear not," said Gobryas; "strike, though it be through both." Darius did as he desired, drove his dagger home, and by good hap killed the Magus.

Thus were the Magi slain; and the seven, cutting off both the heads, and leaving their own wounded in the palace, partly because they were disabled, and partly to guard the citadel, went forth from the gates with the heads in their hands, shouting and making an uproar. They called out to all the Persians whom they met, and told them what had happened, showing them the heads of the Magi, while at the same time they slew every Magus who fell in their way. Then the Persians, when they knew what the seven had done, and understood the fraud of the Magi, thought it but just to follow the example set them, and, drawing their daggers, they killed the Magi wherever they could find any. Such was their fury, that, unless night had closed in, not a single Magus would have been left alive. The Persians observe this day with one accord, and keep it more strictly than any other in the whole year. It is then that they hold the great festival, which they call the Magophonia. No Magus may show himself abroad during the whole time that the feast lasts; but all must remain at home the entire day.

After this the six [the seven conspirators minus Otanes, as he did not wish to be ruled or ruler] took counsel together, as to the fairest way of setting up a king: and first, with respect to Otanes, they resolved, that if any of their own number got the kingdom, Otanes and his seed after him should receive year by year, as a mark of special honour, a Median robe, and all such other gifts as are accounted the most honourable in Persia. And these they resolved to give him, because he was the man who first planned the outbreak, and who brought the seven together. These privileges, therefore, were assigned specially to Otanes. The following were made common to them all: It was to be free to each, whenever he pleased, to enter the palace unannounced, unless the king were in the company of one of his wives; and the king was to be bound to marry into no family excepting those of the conspirators. Concerning the appointment of a king, the resolve to which they came was the following: They would ride out together next morning into the skirts of the city, and he whose steed first neighed after the sun was up should have the kingdom.

Now Darius had a groom, a sharp-witted knave, called Oebares. After the meeting had broken up, Darius sent for him, and said, "Oebares, this is the way in which the king is to be chosen- we are to mount our horses, and the man whose horse first neighs after the sun is up is to have the kingdom. If then you have any cleverness, contrive a plan whereby the prize may fall to us, and not go to another."

"Truly, master," Oebares answered, "if it depends on this whether thou shalt be king or no, set thine heart at ease, and fear nothing: I have a charm which is sure not to fail."

"If thou hast really aught of the kind," said Darius, "hasten to get it ready. The matter does not brook delay, for the trial is to be to-morrow."

So Oebares when he heard that, did as follows: When night came, he took one of the mares, the chief favourite of the horse which Darius rode, and tethering it in the suburb, brought his master's horse to the place; then, after leading him round and round the mare several times, nearer and nearer at each circuit, he ended by letting them come together.

And now, when the morning broke, the six Persians, according to agreement, met together on horseback, and rode out to the suburb. As they went along they neared the spot where the mare was tethered the night before, whereupon the horse of Darius sprang forward and neighed. Just at the same time, though the sky was clear and bright, there was a flash of lightning, followed by a thunderclap. It seemed as if the heavens conspired with Darius, and hereby inaugurated him king: so the five other nobles leaped with one accord from their steeds, and bowed down before him and owned him for their king.[25]

As for deciding which man would be king, the story is probably more myth than fact, and the truth is most likely that Darius was selected as king because of his lineage to a former king of Persia, his grandfather, Arsames. Arsames was the former vassal king of Persia to the king of Mede, Astyages, before Cyrus.

Greek Government & the Jewish Temple Revisited

In the year 521 BC, in Sparta, a baby was born to Anaxandridas II and named Leonidas. Leonidas would be the king of Sparta starting around 489/488 BC. In Athens, the government was under tyrant rule, which simply means that someone illegally seized executive power during a crisis. In an effort to eliminate the tyrants from Athens, the Athenians requested assistance from the Spartan king. To convince the Spartans to help them, they bribed the oracle to say to the Spartans that they must help Athens. Coming from the oracle, how could they refuse? One such tyrant deposed from Athens was Hippias, who was forced to leave by the king of Sparta, Cleomenes. Many of these tyrants would seek the Persians' help against forces seeking to remove them, and it was Hippias that would lead the Persians into the battle at Marathon.

During the sovereignty of Darius, Zorobabel, who had been appointed governor of the Jews that had been in captivity, came to Darius from Jerusalem; for there had been an old friendship between him and the king. He was also, with two others, thought worthy to be guard of the king's body; and obtained that honor which he hoped for. After a test of wisdom, Zorobabel requested that Darius remember and keep the vow that was made by King Cyrus. Now this vow was, "to rebuild Jerusalem, and to build therein the temple of God; and also to restore the vessels which Nebuchadnezzar had pillaged, and carried to Babylon."[26]

 A scroll was found in the citadel of Ecbatana in the province of Media, and this was written on it.

Memorandum:

In the first year of King Cyrus, the king issued a decree concerning the temple of God in Jerusalem:

Let the temple be rebuilt as a place to present sacrifices, and let its foundations be laid. It is to be ninety feet high and ninety feet wide, with three courses of large stones and one of timbers. The costs are to be paid by the royal treasury. Also, the gold and silver articles of the house of God, which Nebuchadnezzar took from the temple in Jerusalem and brought to Babylon, are to be returned to their places in the temple in Jerusalem; they are to be deposited in the house of God.

Now then, Tattenai, governor of Trans-Euphrates, and Shethar-Bozenai and you, their fellow officials of that province, stay away from there. Do not interfere with the work on this temple of God. Let the governor of the Jews and the Jewish elders rebuild this house of God on its site.

Moreover, I hereby decree what you are to do for these elders of the Jews in the construction of this house of God:

The expenses of these men are to be fully paid out of the royal treasury, from the revenues of Trans-Euphrates, so that the work will not stop. Whatever is needed—young bulls, rams, male lambs for burnt offerings to the God of heaven, and wheat, salt, wine and oil, as requested by the priests in Jerusalem—must be given them daily without fail, so that they may offer sacrifices pleasing to the God of heaven and pray for the well-being of the king and his sons.

Furthermore, I decree that if anyone changes this edict, a beam is to be pulled from his house and he is to be lifted up and impaled on it. And for this crime his house is to be made a pile of rubble. May God, who has caused his Name to dwell there, overthrow any king or people who lifts a hand to change this decree or to destroy this temple in Jerusalem ..."[27]

Ezra 6:2–12 (NIV)

Having found this decree of Cyrus, Darius commands it to be done. The Samaritans are not happy, but must obey the king's commands, and they stay away while the king remains on the throne and the temple is completed.

Ionian Revolt

Near the end of the sixth century BC, in 502 BC, the people of the Ionian region began to revolt against King Darius. It would start with the inhabitants of the Greek island Naxos. This revolt led to the larger Ionian Revolt, and then to the Persian War with Greece. Aristagoras, leader of the city Miletus in the Ionian region, attempted to crush the revolt on Naxos but failed. In an attempt to save himself from the wrath of Persia he began to plan a revolt, against the Persians, with the Milesians and other Ionians. In 499 BC, Aristagoras was supported by most of the citizens and soon the other Ionian cities had also revolted against the Persians, thus beginning the Ionian Revolt.[28] In an attempt to gain the support and assistance of the Spartans, Aristagoras met with the Spartan king.

Cleomenes, however, was still king when Aristagoras, tyrant of Miletus, reached Sparta. At their interview, Aristagoras, according to the report of the Lacedaemonians, produced a bronze tablet, whereupon the whole circuit of the earth was engraved, with all its seas and rivers. Discourse began between the two; and Aristagoras addressed the Spartan king in these words following: "Think it not strange, O King Cleomenes, that I have been at the pains to sail hither; for the posture of affairs, which I will now recount unto thee, made it fitting. Shame and grief is it indeed to none so much as to us, that the sons of the Ionians should have lost their freedom, and come to be the slaves of others; but yet it touches you likewise, O Spartans, beyond the rest of the Greeks, inasmuch as the pre-eminence over all Greece appertains to you. We beseech you, therefore, by the common gods of the Grecians, deliver the Ionians, who are your own kinsmen, from slavery. Truly the task is not difficult; for the barbarians are an unwarlike people; and you are the best and bravest warriors in the whole world. Their mode of fighting is the following: they use bows and arrows and a short spear; they wear trousers in the field, and cover their heads with turbans. So easy are they to vanquish! Know too that the dwellers in these parts have more good things than all the rest of the world put together- gold, and silver, and brass, and embroidered garments, beasts of burthen, and bond-servants- all which, if you only wish it, you may soon have for your own. The nations border on one another, in the order which I will now explain. Next to these Ionians" (here he pointed with his finger to the map of the world which was engraved upon the tablet that he had brought with him) "these Lydians dwell; their soil is fertile, and few people are so rich in silver. Next to them," he continued, "come these

Phrygians, who have more flocks and herds than any race that I know, and more plentiful harvests. On them border the Cappadocians, whom we Greeks know by the name of Syrians: they are neighbours to the Cilicians, who extend all the way to this sea, where Cyprus (the island which you see here) lies. The Cilicians pay the king a yearly tribute of five hundred talents. Next to them come the Armenians, who live here- they too have numerous flocks and herds. After them come the Matieni, inhabiting this country; then Cissia, this province, where you see the river Choaspes marked, and likewise the town Susa upon its banks, where the Great King holds his court, and where the treasuries are in which his wealth is stored. Once masters of this city, you may be bold to vie with Jove himself for riches. In the wars which ye wage with your rivals of Messenia, with them of Argos likewise and of Arcadia, about paltry boundaries and strips of land not so remarkably good, ye contend with those who have no gold, nor silver even, which often give men heart to fight and die. Must ye wage such wars, and when ye might so easily be lords of Asia, will ye decide otherwise?" Thus spoke Aristagoras; and Cleomenes replied to him, "Milesian stranger, three days hence I will give thee an answer."

So they proceeded no further at that time. When, however, the day appointed for the answer came, and the two once more met, Cleomenes asked Aristagoras, "how many days' journey is it from the sea of the Ionians to the king's residence?"

Hereupon Aristagoras, who had managed the rest so cleverly, and succeeded in deceiving the king, tripped in his speech and blundered; for instead of concealing the truth, as he ought to have done if he wanted to induce the Spartans to cross into Asia, he said plainly that it was a journey of three months. Cleomenes caught at the words, and, preventing Aristagoras from finishing what he had begun to say concerning the road, addressed him thus: "Milesian stranger, quit Sparta before sunset. This is no good proposal that thou makest to the Lacedaemonians, to conduct them a distance of three months' journey from the sea." When he had thus spoken, Cleomenes went to his home.[29]

Cleomenes turned Aristagoras down because the distance is too far from the sea. The Ionian revolt would have to manage without the help of the Spartans, but the Athenians would assist them. The revolt was put down in 494 BC. In 492 BC, Darius sent Mardonius to Europe to strengthen Persia's hold on Thrace and Macedon, which had been weakened by the Ionian Revolt. In 490 BC, King Darius of Persia made a full-scale attempt to conquer Greece and incorporate it into the Persian Empire, which would secure the weakest portion of his western border.

Having strengthened Thrace and Macedon, in 490 BC the forces of Persia landed in Marathon Bay. Darius wanted to punish the Athenians for their participation in the Ionian revolt. Despite their large numbers, the Persian army was defeated by a small force of Athenians and Plataean heavy infantryman.

The Olympic event known as the "marathon" was inspired by the messenger, Pheidippides, who ran from the battle of Marathon to Athens to announce the victory over the Persians. It is said that he ran the entire distance without stopping and collapsed after announcing to the Athenian Senate, "We have won." Before Darius could finish preparations for another attack against Greece, his attention was turned to an insurrection in Egypt in 486 BC, but he died the next year, 485 BC, and his son Xerxes would ascend to the throne. Xerxes' ascension to the throne was not without conflict. Darius had two wives, each giving him a son. His first wife bore him a son before he became the king. His second wife bore him Xerxes after he became king. The custom of ascension says that the king's firstborn son was heir to the throne. Xerxes was not Darius' firstborn son, but the keywords are "king's" firstborn son. Xerxes was the first son born after Darius became king, making him, by a technicality, the heir to the throne.

Xerxes

During Xerxes' reign, the Samaritans would continue to petition the king to stop the re-building of the city of Jerusalem; however, Xerxes' attention was on Egypt.

But Mardonius, the son of Gobryas, who was at the court, and had more influence with him than any of the other Persians, being his own cousin, the child of a sister of Darius, plied him with discourses like the following:

"Master, it is not fitting that they of Athens escape scot-free, after doing the Persians such great injury. Complete the work which thou hast now in hand, and then, when the pride of Egypt is brought low, lead an army against Athens. So shalt thou thyself have good report among men, and others shall fear hereafter to attack thy country."

Thus far it was of vengeance that he spoke of; but sometimes he would vary the theme, and observe by the way, "that Europe was a wondrous beautiful region, rich in all kinds of cultivated trees, and the soil excellent: no one, save the king, was worthy to own such a land."[30]

It was in Xerxes' third year of reign, 483 BC, that he gave a banquet for all his nobles and officials. The military leaders of Persia and Media, the princes, and the nobles of the provinces were present.

{ For a full 180 days he displayed the vast wealth of his kingdom and the splendor and glory of his majesty. When these days were over, the king gave a banquet, lasting seven days, in the enclosed garden of the king's palace, for all the people from the least to the greatest, who were in the citadel of Susa. The garden had hangings of white and blue linen, fastened with cords of white linen and purple material to silver rings on marble pillars. There were couches of gold and silver on a mosaic pavement of porphyry, marble, mother-of-pearl and other costly stones. Wine was served in goblets of gold, each one different from the other, and the royal wine was abundant in keeping with the king's liberality. By the king's command each guest was allowed to drink in his own way, for the king instructed all the wine stewards to serve each man what he wished. Queen Vashti also gave a banquet for the women in the royal palace of King Xerxes.

On the seventh day, when King Xerxes was in high spirits from wine, he commanded the seven eunuchs who served him—Mehuman, Biztha, Harbona, Bigtha, Abagtha, Zethar and Carcas-to bring before him Queen Vashti, wearing her royal crown, in order to display her beauty to the people and nobles, for she was lovely to look at. But when the attendants delivered the king's command, Queen Vashti refused to come. Then the king became furious and burned with anger.

Since it was customary for the king to consult experts in matters of law and justice, he spoke with the wise men who understood the times and were closest to the king—Carshena, Shethar, Admatha, Tarshish, Meres, Marsena and Memucan, the seven nobles of Persia and Media who had special access to the king and were highest in the kingdom.

"According to law, what must be done to Queen Vashti?" he asked. "She has not obeyed the command of King Xerxes that the eunuchs have taken to her."

Then Memucan replied in the presence of the king and the nobles, "Queen Vashti has done wrong, not only against the king but also against all the nobles and the peoples of all the provinces of King Xerxes. For the queen's conduct will become known to all the women, and so they will despise their husbands and say, 'King Xerxes commanded Queen Vashti to be brought before him, but she would not come.' This very day the Persian and Median women of the nobility who have heard about the queen's conduct will respond to all the king's nobles in the same way. There will be no end of disrespect and discord.

"Therefore, if it pleases the king, let him issue a royal decree and let it be written in the laws of

Persia and Media, which cannot be repealed, that Vashti is never again to enter the presence of King Xerxes. Also let the king give her royal position to someone else who is better than she. Then when the king's edict is proclaimed throughout all his vast realm, all the women will respect their husbands, from the least to the greatest."

The king and his nobles were pleased with this advice, so the king did as Memucan proposed. He sent dispatches to all parts of the kingdom, to each province in its own script and to each people in its own language, proclaiming in each people's tongue that every man should be ruler over his own household.

Later when the anger of King Xerxes had subsided, he remembered Vashti and what she had done and what he had decreed about her. Then the king's personal attendants proposed, "Let a search be made for beautiful young virgins for the king. Let the king appoint commissioners in every province of his realm to bring all these beautiful girls into the harem at the citadel of Susa. Let them be placed under the care of Hegai, the king's eunuch, who is in charge of the women; and let beauty treatments be given to them. Then let the girl who pleases the king be queen instead of Vashti." This advice appealed to the king, and he followed it.

Esther 1–2:4

Satisfied with this action, Xerxes turns his full attention to the plans against the Greek nation. In the year 480 BC, he encounters them at the battle of Thermopylae against the Spartan king, Leonidas. The search for a new queen continues in his absence. It is possible that these virgins were taken to Xerxes on the battle field during his encounters with the Greeks, after the women fulfilled their year of purification.

The Battle at Thermopylae lasted about four days before Xerxes' army defeated the Greeks and their allies led by Spartan king, Leonidas. Xerxes then took his army into Athens, which had been evacuated (some Athenians went to Egina, some to Salamis, but the greater number to Troezen) and destroyed the city, revenging his father's defeat by the Athenians at Marathon.

A few Athenian men remained in Athens and barricaded themselves inside the citadel with planks and boards. They believed the oracle's promise that "the wooden wall should never be taken" meant the wall they had built. Xerxes stationed his army on the hill against the citadel, the hill known as Mars Hill, then overtook and burned the citadel. The next day he collected together all the Athenian exiles that had come into Greece in his train, and told them to go up into the citadel and there offer sacrifice after their own fashion.

The Greeks retreated their fleet of ships into the bay near Salamis. Xerxes requested the advice of his generals as to whether he should follow them. Only one speaks up against following the Greeks into the bay of Salamis: Artemisia, a female ruler of Halicarnassus in Asia Minor and Persian ally commanding five ships. When asked if they should pursue a sea battle against the Greeks, Artemisia advised Xerxes:

"O my lord, to tell thee plainly what I think to be most for thy advantage now. This then is my advice. Spare thy ships, and do not risk a battle; for these people are as much superior to thy people in seamanship, as men to women. What so great need is there for thee to incur hazard at sea? Art thou not master of Athens, for which thou didst undertake thy expedition?"[31]

Xerxes follows in spite of Artemisia's recommendation. The Persians were unsuccessful and their fleet was defeated. After this defeat, Artemisia convinced Xerxes to retreat back to Asia Minor and Xerxes returns to Susa, satisfied in having burned Athens. His armies continued the fight until the final battle of the Greco-Persian wars in Plataea in 479 BC. Meanwhile, back in Susa, the search for a new queen to replace Vashti continued and in Xerxes' sixth year, 479 BC:

> Now there was in the citadel of Susa a Jew of the tribe of Benjamin, named Mordecai son of Jair, the son of Shimei, the son of Kish, who had been carried into exile from Jerusalem by Nebuchadnezzar king of Babylon, among those taken captive with Jehoiachin king of Judah.
>
> Esther 2:5–6

There has been a lot of controversy over this story of Esther. It has been suggested that Xerxes was not the king at the time of Esther, that this story probably took place during a later king's reign. The book of Esther uses the name "Ahasuerus" in the King James Version. Some scholars suggest this is Artexerxes and not Xerxes. This passage in Esther says that Kish was carried into exile from Jerusalem when Jehoiachin was taken captive. So let's do some math: Jehoiachin was in prison for thirty-seven years, and released when Amel-Marduk took the throne. Amel-Marduk reigned for two years. After him, Neriglissar reigned for four years. Labashi-Marduk reigned a few months. Nabonidus was on the throne for seventeen years when Cyrus invaded. Cyrus was King for ten years after taking Babylon and succeeded by his son Cambyses II, who reigned for seven years. Darius was king for thirty-six years. Xerxes takes the throne and, assuming Xerxes was the king when Esther's story occurred, the number of years that passed from the time Jehoiachin was put in prison until Esther had her "night with the king" in his seventh year:

$$37+2+4+17+10+7+36+7=120 \text{ years.}$$

Let us assume Shimei was not born when Jehoiachin was put in prison, because the Bible says that Kish was carried into exile. It does not say that Shimei was carried into exile. For the sake of argument, let us also assume that Shimei was born that same year of the exile. Giving each man the age of forty when the next was born, if Shimei is forty when Jair is born and Jair is forty when Mordecai is born, then Mordecai is forty when Esther has her night with Xerxes, in his seventh year of reign.

40+40+40=120 years

Xerxes was king for twenty years and Artexerxes I was king for forty years. We can go on and on, but placing this story in the life of any other king would put Mordecai at such an old age that it would be unreasonable to think he had a cousin that was so young. Since Esther was a virgin, she was probably in her late teens or early twenties at best. She was the daughter of Mordecai's uncle, so common sense tells us that this story must have been during Xerxes' reign as king.

Mordecai had a cousin named Hadassah, whom he had brought up because she had neither father nor mother. This girl, who was also known as Esther, was lovely in form and features, and Mordecai had taken her as his own daughter when her father and mother died.

When the king's order and edict had been proclaimed, many girls were brought to the citadel of Susa and put under the care of Hegai. Esther also was taken to the king's palace and entrusted to Hegai, who had charge of the harem. The girl pleased him and won his favor. Immediately he provided her with her beauty treatments and special food. He assigned to her seven maids selected from the king's palace and moved her and her maids into the best place in the harem.

Esther had not revealed her nationality and family background, because Mordecai had forbidden her to do so. Every day he walked back and forth near the courtyard of the harem to find out how Esther was and what was happening to her.

Before a girl's turn came to go in to King Xerxes, she had to complete twelve months of beauty treatments prescribed for the women, six months with oil of myrrh and six with perfumes and cosmetics. And this is how she would go to the king: Anything she wanted was given her to take with her from the harem to the king's palace. In the evening she would go there and in the morning return to another part of the harem to the care of Shaashgaz, the king's eunuch who was in charge of the concubines. She would not return to the king unless he was pleased with her and summoned her by name.

When the turn came for Esther (the girl Mordecai had adopted, the daughter of his uncle Abihail) to go to the king, she asked for nothing other than what Hegai, the king's eunuch who was in charge of the harem, suggested. And Esther won the favor of everyone who saw her. She was taken to King Xerxes in the royal residence in the tenth month, the month of Tebeth, in the seventh year of his reign.

Now the king was attracted to Esther more than to any of the other women, and she won his favor and approval more than any of the other virgins. So he set a royal crown on her head and made her queen instead of Vashti. And the king gave a great banquet, Esther's banquet, for all his nobles and officials. He proclaimed a holiday throughout the provinces and distributed gifts with royal liberality.

When the virgins were assembled a second time, Mordecai was sitting at the king's gate. But Esther had kept secret her family background and nationality just as Mordecai had told her to do, for she continued to follow Mordecai's instructions as she had done when he was bringing her up.

During the time Mordecai was sitting at the king's gate, Bigthana and Teresh, two of the king's officers who guarded the doorway, became angry and conspired to assassinate King Xerxes. But Mordecai found out about the plot and told Queen Esther, who in turn reported it to the king, giving credit to Mordecai. And when the report was investigated and found to be true, the two officials were hanged on a gallows. All this was recorded in the book of the annals in the presence of the king.

After these events, King Xerxes honored Haman son of Hammedatha, the Agagite, elevating him and giving him a seat of honor higher than that of all the other nobles. All the royal officials at the king's gate knelt down and paid honor to Haman, for the king had commanded this concerning him. But Mordecai would not kneel down or pay him honor.

> Then the royal officials at the king's gate asked Mordecai, "Why do you disobey the king's command?" Day after day they spoke to him but he refused to comply. Therefore they told Haman about it to see whether Mordecai's behavior would be tolerated, for he had told them he was a Jew.
>
> When Haman saw that Mordecai would not kneel down or pay him honor, he was enraged. Yet having learned who Mordecai's people were, he scorned the idea of killing only Mordecai. Instead Haman looked for a way to destroy all Mordecai's people, the Jews, throughout the whole kingdom of Xerxes.
>
> Esther 2:5–3:6 (NIV)

After the Persian army left Greece, the people of the Greek cities returned home. The Athenians, who were at Troezen, Aegina and Salamis after the battle of Plataea returned and found their city in total ruin and the countryside desolated. They soon started rebuilding the city and began raising walls (478 BC). Themistocles, the leader of Athens, planned the rebuilding of their navy and the city walls. The balance of power between Athens and Sparta was emphasized through the formation of what would be called the Delian League. Members subscribed to one common naval fleet, either by contributing ships, crews, or money. The Spartans wanted no part of the League because they had little interest in naval warfare.

The Delian League grew in strength and achieved several victories against the Persians in the eastern Aegean. Themistocles began to abuse his power and was accused of accepting bribes. He became arrogant and lost favor with the Athenians. Around 473 BC he was ostracized and new leaders rose up to take over. Themistocles retired to Argos, but the Spartans accused him of treasonable offenses with the Persians so he fled to Corcyra, then to Admetus and Asia Minor. He was proclaimed a traitor in Athens and his property was confiscated. He was eventually offered asylum by Artaxerxes I, successor and son of Xerxes king of Persia, around 461 BC.

Haman's Plot

Themistocles is not the only one with problems. Haman's plan against the Jews is beginning to take shape.

In the twelfth year of King Xerxes, in the first month, the month of Nisan, they cast the pur (that is, the lot) in the presence of Haman to select a day and month. And the lot fell on the twelfth month, the month of Adar.

Then Haman said to King Xerxes, "There is a certain people dispersed and scattered among the peoples in all the provinces of your kingdom whose customs are different from those of all other people and who do not obey the king's laws; it is not in the king's best interest to tolerate them. If it pleases the king, let a decree be issued to destroy them, and I will put ten thousand talents of silver into the royal treasury for the men who carry out this business."

So the king took his signet ring from his finger and gave it to Haman son of Hammedatha, the Agagite, the enemy of the Jews. "Keep the money," the king said to Haman, "and do with the people as you please."

Then on the thirteenth day of the first month the royal secretaries were summoned. They wrote out in the script of each province and in the language of each people all Haman's orders to the king's satraps, the governors of the various provinces and the nobles of the various peoples. These were written in the name of King Xerxes himself and sealed with his own ring. Dispatches were sent by couriers to all the king's provinces with the order to destroy, kill and annihilate all the Jews—young and old, women and little children—on a single day, the thirteenth day of the twelfth month, the month of Adar, and to plunder their goods. A copy of the text of the edict was to be issued as law in every province and made known to the people of every nationality so they would be ready for that day.

Spurred on by the king's command, the couriers went out, and the edict was issued in the citadel of Susa. The king and Haman sat down to drink, but the city of Susa was bewildered.

When Mordecai learned of all that had been done, he tore his clothes, put on sackcloth and ashes, and went out into the city, wailing loudly and bitterly. But he went only as far as the king's gate, because no one clothed in sackcloth was allowed to enter it. In every province to which the edict and order of the king came, there was great mourning among the Jews, with fasting, weeping and wailing. Many lay in sackcloth and ashes.

When Esther's maids and eunuchs came and

told her about Mordecai, she was in great distress. She sent clothes for him to put on instead of his sackcloth, but he would not accept them. Then Esther summoned Hathach, one of the king's eunuchs assigned to attend her, and ordered him to find out what was troubling Mordecai and why.

So Hathach went out to Mordecai in the open square of the city in front of the king's gate. Mordecai told him everything that had happened to him, including the exact amount of money Haman had promised to pay into the royal treasury for the destruction of the Jews. He also gave him a copy of the text of the edict for their annihilation, which had been published in Susa, to show to Esther and explain it to her, and he told him to urge her to go into the king's presence to beg for mercy and plead with him for her people.

Hathach went back and reported to Esther what Mordecai had said. Then she instructed him to say to Mordecai, "All the king's officials and the people of the royal provinces know that for any man or woman who approaches the king in the inner court without being summoned the king has but one law: that he be put to death. The only exception to this is for the king to extend the gold scepter to him and spare his life. But thirty days have passed since I was called to go to the king."

When Esther's words were reported to Mordecai, he sent back this answer: "Do not think that because you are in the king's house you alone of all the Jews will escape. For if you remain silent at this time, relief and deliverance for the Jews will arise from another place, but you and your father's family will perish. And who knows but that you have come to royal position for such a time as this?"

Then Esther sent this reply to Mordecai: "Go, gather together all the Jews who are in Susa, and fast for me. Do not eat or drink for three days, night or day. I and my maids will fast as you do. When this is done, I will go to the king, even though it is against the law. And if I perish, I perish." So Mordecai went away and carried out all of Esther's instructions.

On the third day Esther put on her royal robes and stood in the inner court of the palace, in front of the king's hall. The king was sitting on his royal throne in the hall, facing the entrance. When he saw Queen Esther standing in the court, he was pleased with her and held out to her the gold scepter that was in his hand. So Esther approached and touched the tip of the scepter.

Then the king asked, "What is it, Queen Esther? What is your request? Even up to half the kingdom, it will be given you."

"If it pleases the king," replied Esther, "let

the king, together with Haman, come today to a banquet I have prepared for him."

"Bring Haman at once," the king said, "so that we may do what Esther asks." So the king and Haman went to the banquet Esther had prepared. As they were drinking wine, the king again asked Esther, "Now what is your petition? It will be given you. And what is your request? Even up to half the kingdom, it will be granted."

Esther replied, "My petition and my request is this: If the king regards me with favor and if it pleases the king to grant my petition and fulfill my request, let the king and Haman come tomorrow to the banquet I will prepare for them. Then I will answer the king's question."

Haman went out that day happy and in high spirits. But when he saw Mordecai at the king's gate and observed that he neither rose nor showed fear in his presence, he was filled with rage against Mordecai. Nevertheless, Haman restrained himself and went home. Calling together his friends and Zeresh, his wife, Haman boasted to them about his vast wealth, his many sons, and all the ways the king had honored him and how he had elevated him above the other nobles and officials.

"And that's not all," Haman added. "I'm the only person Queen Esther invited to accompany the king to the banquet she gave. And she has invited me along with the king tomorrow. But all this gives me no satisfaction as long as I see that Jew Mordecai sitting at the king's gate."

His wife Zeresh and all his friends said to him, "Have a gallows built, seventy-five feet high, and ask the king in the morning to have Mordecai hanged on it. Then go with the king to the dinner and be happy." This suggestion delighted Haman, and he had the gallows built.

That night the king could not sleep; so he ordered the book of the chronicles, the record of his reign, to be brought in and read to him. It was found recorded there that Mordecai had exposed Bigthana and Teresh, two of the king's officers who guarded the doorway, who had conspired to assassinate King Xerxes.

"What honor and recognition has Mordecai received for this?" the king asked.

"Nothing has been done for him," his attendants answered.

The king said, "Who is in the court?" Now Haman had just entered the outer court of the palace to speak to the king about hanging Mordecai on the gallows he had erected for him.

His attendants answered, "Haman is standing in the court."

"Bring him in," the king ordered.

When Haman entered, the king asked him, "What should be done for the man the king delights to honor?"

Now Haman thought to himself, "Who is there that the king would rather honor than me?" So he answered the king, "For the man the king delights to honor, have them bring a royal robe the king has worn and a horse the king has ridden, one with a royal crest placed on its head. Then let the robe and horse be entrusted to one of the king's most noble princes. Let them robe the man the king delights to honor, and lead him on the horse through the city streets, proclaiming before him, 'This is what is done for the man the king delights to honor!' "

"Go at once," the king commanded Haman. "Get the robe and the horse and do just as you have suggested for Mordecai the Jew, who sits at the king's gate. Do not neglect anything you have recommended."

So Haman got the robe and the horse. He robed Mordecai, and led him on horseback through the city streets, proclaiming before him, "This is what is done for the man the king delights to honor!"

Afterward Mordecai returned to the king's gate. But Haman rushed home, with his head covered in grief, and told Zeresh his wife and all his friends everything that had happened to him.

His advisers and his wife Zeresh said to him, "Since Mordecai, before whom your downfall has started, is of Jewish origin, you cannot stand against him—you will surely come to ruin!" While they were still talking with him, the king's eunuchs arrived and hurried Haman away to the banquet Esther had prepared.

So the king and Haman went to dine with Queen Esther, and as they were drinking wine on that second day, the king again asked, "Queen Esther, what is your petition? It will be given you. What is your request? Even up to half the kingdom, it will be granted."

Then Queen Esther answered, "If I have found favor with you, O king, and if it pleases your majesty, grant me my life—this is my petition. And spare my people—this is my request. For I and my people have been sold for destruction and slaughter and annihilation. If we had merely been sold as male and female slaves, I would have kept quiet, because no such distress would justify disturbing the king."

King Xerxes asked Queen Esther, "Who is he? Where is the man who has dared to do such a thing?"

Esther said, "The adversary and enemy is this vile Haman."

Then Haman was terrified before the king and queen. The king got up in a rage, left his wine and went out into the palace garden. But Haman, realizing that the king had already decided his fate, stayed behind to beg Queen Esther for his life.

Just as the king returned from the palace garden to the banquet hall, Haman was falling on the couch where Esther was reclining.

The king exclaimed, "Will he even molest the queen while she is with me in the house?"

As soon as the word left the king's mouth, they covered Haman's face. Then Harbona, one of the eunuchs attending the king, said, "A gallows seventy-five feet high stands by Haman's house. He had it made for Mordecai, who spoke up to help the king."

The king said, "Hang him on it!" So they hanged Haman on the gallows he had prepared for Mordecai. Then the king's fury subsided.

That same day King Xerxes gave Queen Esther the estate of Haman, the enemy of the Jews. And Mordecai came into the presence of the king, for Esther had told how he was related to her. The king took off his signet ring, which he had reclaimed from Haman, and presented it to Mordecai. And Esther appointed him over Haman's estate.

Esther again pleaded with the king, falling at his feet and weeping. She begged him to put an end to the evil plan of Haman the Agagite, which he had devised against the Jews. Then the king extended the gold scepter to Esther and she arose and stood before him.

"If it pleases the king," she said, "and if he regards me with favor and thinks it the right thing to do, and if he is pleased with me, let an order be written overruling the dispatches that Haman son of Hammedatha, the Agagite, devised and wrote to destroy the Jews in all the king's provinces. For how can I bear to see disaster fall on my people? How can I bear to see the destruction of my family?"

King Xerxes replied to Queen Esther and to Mordecai the Jew, "Because Haman attacked the Jews, I have given his estate to Esther, and they have hanged him on the gallows. Now write another decree in the king's name in behalf of the Jews as seems best to you, and seal it with the king's signet ring—for no document written in the king's name and sealed with his ring can be revoked."

At once the royal secretaries were summoned—on the twenty-third day of the third month, the month of Sivan. They wrote out all Mordecai's orders to the Jews, and to the satraps, governors and nobles of the 127 provinces stretching from India to Cush. These orders were written in the script of each province and the language of each people and also to the Jews in their own script and language. Mordecai wrote in the name of King Xerxes, sealed the dispatches with the king's signet ring, and sent them by mounted couriers, who rode fast horses especially bred for the king.

The king's edict granted the Jews in every

city the right to assemble and protect themselves; to destroy, kill and annihilate any armed force of any nationality or province that might attack them and their women and children; and to plunder the property of their enemies. The day appointed for the Jews to do this in all the provinces of King Xerxes was the thirteenth day of the twelfth month, the month of Adar. A copy of the text of the edict was to be issued as law in every province and made known to the people of every nationality so that the Jews would be ready on that day to avenge themselves on their enemies.

The couriers, riding the royal horses, raced out, spurred on by the king's command. And the edict was also issued in the citadel of Susa.

Mordecai left the king's presence wearing royal garments of blue and white, a large crown of gold and a purple robe of fine linen. And the city of Susa held a joyous celebration. For the Jews it was a time of happiness and joy, gladness and honor. In every province and in every city, wherever the edict of the king went, there was joy and gladness among the Jews, with feasting and celebrating. And many people of other nationalities became Jews because fear of the Jews had seized them.

On the thirteenth day of the twelfth month, the month of Adar, the edict commanded by the king was to be carried out. On this day the enemies of the Jews had hoped to overpower them, but now the tables were turned and the Jews got the upper hand over those who hated them. The Jews assembled in their cities in all the provinces of King Xerxes to attack those seeking their destruction. No one could stand against them, because the people of all the other nationalities were afraid of them. And all the nobles of the provinces, the satraps, the governors and the king's administrators helped the Jews, because fear of Mordecai had seized them. Mordecai was prominent in the palace; his reputation spread throughout the provinces, and he became more and more powerful.

The Jews struck down all their enemies with the sword, killing and destroying them, and they did what they pleased to those who hated them. In the citadel of Susa, the Jews killed and destroyed five hundred men. They also killed Parshandatha, Dalphon, Aspatha, Poratha, Adalia, Aridatha, Parmashta, Arisai, Aridai and Vaizatha, the ten sons of Haman son of Hammedatha, the enemy of the Jews. But they did not lay their hands on the plunder.

The number of those slain in the citadel of Susa was reported to the king that same day. The king said to Queen Esther, "The Jews have killed and destroyed five hundred men and the ten sons of Haman in the citadel of Susa. What have they done in the rest of the king's provinces? Now what is your petition? It will be given you. What is your request? It will also be granted."

"If it pleases the king," Esther answered, "give the Jews in Susa permission to carry out this day's edict tomorrow also, and let Haman's ten sons be hanged on gallows."

So the king commanded that this be done. An edict was issued in Susa, and they hanged the ten sons of Haman. The Jews in Susa came together on the fourteenth day of the month of Adar, and they put to death in Susa three hundred men, but they did not lay their hands on the plunder.

Meanwhile, the remainder of the Jews who were in the king's provinces also assembled to protect themselves and get relief from their enemies. They killed seventy-five thousand of them but did not lay their hands on the plunder. This happened on the thirteenth day of the month of Adar, and on the fourteenth they rested and made it a day of feasting and joy.

The Jews in Susa, however, had assembled on the thirteenth and fourteenth, and then on the fifteenth they rested and made it a day of feasting and joy.

That is why rural Jews—those living in villages—observe the fourteenth of the month of Adar as a day of joy and feasting, a day for giving presents to each other.

Mordecai recorded these events, and he sent letters to all the Jews throughout the provinces of

King Xerxes, near and far, to have them celebrate annually the fourteenth and fifteenth days of the month of Adar as the time when the Jews got relief from their enemies, and as the month when their sorrow was turned into joy and their mourning into a day of celebration. He wrote them to observe the days as days of feasting and joy and giving presents of food to one another and gifts to the poor.

So the Jews agreed to continue the celebration they had begun, doing what Mordecai had written to them. For Haman son of Hammedatha, the Agagite, the enemy of all the Jews, had plotted against the Jews to destroy them and had cast the pur (that is, the lot) for their ruin and destruction. But when the plot came to the king's attention, he issued written orders that the evil scheme Haman had devised against the Jews should come back onto his own head, and that he and his sons should be hanged on the gallows. (Therefore these days were called Purim, from the word pur.) Because of everything written in this letter and because of what they had seen and what had happened to them, the Jews took it upon themselves to establish the custom that they and their descendants and all who join them should without fail observe these two days every year, in the way prescribed and at the time appointed. These days should be remembered and observed in every generation by every family, and in every province and in every city. And these days of Purim should never cease to be celebrated by the Jews, nor should the memory of them die out among their descendants.

So Queen Esther, daughter of Abihail, along with Mordecai the Jew, wrote with full authority to confirm this second letter concerning Purim. And Mordecai sent letters to all the Jews in the 127 provinces of the kingdom of Xerxes—words of goodwill and assurance- to establish these days of Purim at their designated times, as Mordecai the Jew and Queen Esther had decreed for them, and as they had established for themselves and their descendants in regard to their times of fasting and lamentation. Esther's decree confirmed these regulations about Purim, and it was written down in the records.

King Xerxes imposed tribute throughout the empire, to its distant shores. And all his acts of power and might, together with a full account of the greatness of Mordecai to which the king had raised him, are they not written in the book of the annals of the kings of Media and Persia?

Mordecai the Jew was second in rank to King Xerxes, preeminent among the Jews, and held in high esteem by his many fellow Jews, because he worked for the good of his people and spoke up for the welfare of all the Jews.

Esther 3–10 (NIV) }

With the power of Mordecai in the Persian Empire and the Jewish Queen Esther, Judaism and the worship of their God spread throughout the empire. "And many people of other nationalities became Jews because fear of the Jews had seized them." (Esther 8:17, NIV)

Socrates

Around the year 470 BC, in Athens, was born a child named Socrates. He was the son of the statuary Sophroniscus and of the midwife Phaenarete. As a youth he received the customary instruction in gymnastics and music. He also made himself acquainted with geometry, astronomy, and the methods and the doctrines of the leaders of Greek thought and culture, which included the Pythagorean doctrines. The Athenian government was still uncertain and wars were occurring. The city was being rebuilt and the population was growing.

The Athenians began to treat their Delian League allies unfairly. They forcibly retained members and demanded annual dues instead of ships. In 465 BC, in Persia, Xerxes is murdered and his son, Artaxerxes I, ascends to the throne of Persia. Around 461 BC, Pericles rises up to lead Athens. 454 BC the funds that were collected for the Delian League and stored in Delos were transferred to Athens. Pericles turned the Delian League into an Athenian empire and Athens quickly drew the attention and concern of Sparta. They rebuilt their walls and extended them 5 miles to include their harbor at Piraeus. Sparta has no city walls. With the most powerful navy in Greece, and a fortified city and harbor, the Athenians are unmistakably presenting themselves as the dominant power of the region. Pericles initiated an ambitious building project which lasted the entire second half of the fifth century BC. In 447 BC, the Athenians began to re-build the Parthenon that was destroyed by Xerxes in 480 BC. They used some of the funds from the Delian League for this reconstruction, which lasted until 431 BC. Other buildings constructed were the Propylaia, the Erechtheion and the temple of Athena Nike.

Socrates began life as a sculptor and mason, but he soon abandoned the art and gave himself to what may best be called education. He may have been paid to assist in these constructions. It has been thought that Socrates crafted the statues of the Three Graces, which stood near the Acropolis until the second century AD. Socrates, however, preferred to engage his mind in the philosophies of life and divinities.

Athens was not the only city to be concerned with rebuilding. In Jerusalem, the walls were still unfinished and in rubble. Around 458 BC, Ezra left Babylon and approached Artaxerxes king of Persia. This is the decree given to Ezra by Artaxerxes:

Artaxerxes, king of kings, To Ezra the priest, a teacher of the Law of the God of heaven: Greetings.

Now I decree that any of the Israelites in my kingdom, including priests and Levites, who wish to go to Jerusalem with you, may go. You are sent by the king and his seven advisers to inquire about Judah and Jerusalem with regard to the Law of your God, which is in your hand.

Moreover, you are to take with you the silver and
gold that the king and his advisers have freely
given to the God of Israel, whose dwelling is in
Jerusalem, together with all the silver and gold
you may obtain from the province of Babylon,
as well as the freewill offerings of the people and
priests for the temple of their God in Jerusalem.
With this money be sure to buy bulls, rams and
male lambs, together with their grain offerings
and drink offerings, and sacrifice them on the
altar of the temple of your God in Jerusalem.

You and your brother Jews may then do
whatever seems best with the rest of the silver
and gold, in accordance with the will of your God.
Deliver to the God of Jerusalem all the articles
entrusted to you for worship in the temple of your
God. And anything else needed for the temple of
your God that you may have occasion to supply,
you may provide from the royal treasury.

Now I, King Artaxerxes, order all the
treasurers of Trans-Euphrates to provide with
diligence whatever Ezra the priest, a teacher of
the Law of the God of heaven, may ask of you -
up to a hundred talents of silver, a hundred cors of
wheat, a hundred baths of wine, a hundred baths
of olive oil, and salt without limit. Whatever the
God of heaven has prescribed let it be done with
diligence for the temple of the God of heaven.
Why should there be wrath against the realm of
the king and of his sons? You are also to know

> that you have no authority to impose taxes, tribute or duty on any of the priests, Levites, singers, gatekeepers, temple servants or other workers at this house of God.
>
> And you, Ezra, in accordance with the wisdom of your God, which you possess, appoint magistrates and judges to administer justice to all the people of Trans-Euphrates—all who know the laws of your God. And you are to teach any who do not know them. Whoever does not obey the law of your God and the law of the king must surely be punished by death, banishment, confiscation of property, or imprisonment.
>
> Ezra 7:12–26 (NIV)

Ezra was not the only one to go to Jerusalem to assist in the efforts. Nehemiah, who was a cupbearer in the king's palace, approached King Artaxerxes and requested permission to go to Jerusalem in 445 BC. It was Nehemiah that masterminded the construction of the city walls. The Samaritans and their allies did not like that the city walls were being rebuilt in Jerusalem any more than the Spartans liked the walls of Athens rebuilt. The distrust between Sparta and Athens would eventually lead to the Peloponnesian War, which started in 431 BC and lasted until 404 BC. Socrates would have been around thirty-nine years old when this war began, his formal education being over and his search for new wisdom beginning. A primary source of formal education was the Pythagoreans.

They were well-versed in the areas of geometry and astronomy. Pythagoras was the first to call himself a philosopher, or lover of wisdom. Socrates was familiar with and educated in the philosophies of Pythagoras. Although not considered a Pythagorean, he learned about the Jews and their laws that were integrated into Pythagoras' teachings. Like Pythagoras, Socrates was a sponge soaking up knowledge and seeking new ideas. Perhaps it was through Pythagoras that Socrates learned about and believed as well that the earth was a sphere, as he explained it in the dialogues of Plato's "Phaedo":

"What do you mean, Socrates? said Simmias. I have myself heard many descriptions of the earth, but I do not know, and I should very much like to know, in which of these you put faith.

And I, Simmias, replied Socrates, if I had the art of Glaucus would tell you; although I know not that the art of Glaucus could prove the truth of my tale, which I myself should never be able to prove, and even if I could, I fear, Simmias, that my life would come to an end before the argument was completed. I may describe to you, however, the form and regions of the earth according to my conception of them.

That, said Simmias, will be enough.

Well, then, he said, my conviction is, *that the earth is a round body in the centre of the heavens*, and therefore has no need of air or any similar force to be a support, but is kept there and hindered from falling or inclining any way by the equability of the surrounding heaven and by her own equipoise. For that which, being in equipoise, is in the centre of that which is equably diffused, will not incline any way in any degree, but will always remain in the same state and not deviate. And this is my first notion.

"Which is surely a correct one," said Simmias.

"Also I believe that the earth is very vast, and that we who dwell in the region extending from the river Phasis to the Pillars of Heracles inhabit a small portion only about the sea, like ants or frogs about a marsh, and that there are other inhabitants of many other like places; for everywhere on the face of the earth there are hollows of various forms and sizes, into which the water and the mist and the lower air collect. But the true earth is pure and situated in the pure heaven—there are the stars also; and it is the heaven which is commonly spoken of by us as the ether, and of which our own earth is the sediment gathering in the hollows beneath. But we who live in these hollows are deceived into the notion that we are dwelling above on the surface of the earth; which is just as if a creature who was at the bottom of the sea were to fancy that he was on the surface of the water, and that the sea was the heaven through which he saw the sun and the other stars, he having never come to the surface by reason of his feebleness and sluggishness, and having never lifted up his head and seen, nor ever heard from one who had seen, how much purer and fairer the world above is than his own. And such is exactly our case: for we are dwelling in a hollow of the earth, and fancy that we are on the surface; and the air we call the heaven, in which we imagine that the stars move. But the fact is, that owing to our feebleness and sluggishness we are prevented from reaching the surface of the air: for if any man could arrive at the exterior limit, or take the wings of a bird and come to the top, then like a fish who puts his head out of the water and sees this world, he would see a world beyond; and, if the nature of man could sustain the sight, he would acknowledge that this other world was the place of the true heaven and the true light and the true earth."[32]

With such an open mind, Socrates was eager to study science, philosophy and religion. Judaism had spread throughout Persia and had filtered into Greece. Socrates learned of the Jewish people that were known as prophets. These prophets heard directly from God and prophesied to the Jewish people. This was not the way of the Greeks. They went to the Oracle, and the oracle heard from the gods. Socrates explained in Plato's *Apology* that he heard directly from God from the time he was a child: "This sign I have had ever since I was a child. The sign is a voice that comes to me and always forbids me to do something which I am going to do, but never commands me to do anything."[33]

In Xenophon's *Apology of Socrates*, Socrates says:

> And as to novel divinities, how, pray, am I supposed to introduce them by stating that I have a voice from God which clearly signifies to me what I ought to do? Why, what else do those who make use of the cries of birds or utterances of men draw their conclusions from if not from voices? Who will deny that the thunder has a voice and is a very mighty omen; and the priestess on her tripod at Pytho, does not she also proclaim by voice the messages from the god? The god, at any rate, has foreknowledge, and premonishes those whom he will of what is about to be. That is a thing which all the world believes and asserts even as I do. Only, when they describe these premonitions under the name of birds and utterances, tokens and soothsayers, I speak of a divinity, and in using that designation I claim to speak at once more exactly and more reverentially than they do who ascribe the power of the gods to birds. And that I am not lying against the Godhead I have this as a proof: although I have reported to numbers of friends the counsels of heaven, I have never at any time been shown to be a deceiver or deceived.[34]

Socrates "has reported to numbers of friends the counsels of heaven…" He has prophesied to his friends that which was told to him by God. These are the characteristics that the mind of Socrates has studied and learned from the Pythagoreans and the Jews he encountered in his youth and developed throughout his life, even in the face of criticism. Socrates knows of the prophets of the Jews, he is told about Daniel the leader of the Chaldean Magi. He knows of Mordecai and the Persian Queen. He knows of Jerusalem and the rebuilding efforts there; so, he knows of Ezra and Nehemiah, Zechariah, and Haggai. He is educated in the history of the Athenian enemies as well as the history of Athens. Athens is going through a state of re-building his entire life. As a sculptor, Socrates himself contributes to the efforts.

Socrates begins to receive criticisms from his fellow citizens. They call him: "…a curious person, who searches into things under the earth and in heaven, and he makes the worse appear the better cause; and he teaches the aforesaid doctrines to others."[35] In the play written by Aristophanes sometime around 423 BC, this same statement is used.[36] By reading this play, we can assume the meaning of this accusation. The play tells us about a "well to do" man, Strepsiades, that has fallen to troubled times. He tells his son, Phidippides, to go and get educated in the area of lawsuits. Phidippides refuses to go and Strepsiades ends up at the school to learn the skills of lawsuits for himself. At the school, Strepsiades enters to see the students staring at the ground. He asks "…why do they look so fixedly on the ground?"

The answer comes back, "They are seeking for what is below the ground."

Then he sees students staring into the sky and asks, "And what are they looking at in the heavens?"

To which the answer is, "They are studying astronomy on their own account."

Strepsiades then comes in to find Socrates suspended in a basket and asks why he is up there. Socrates (the character in the play, not the real Socrates) tells him that he is up there to "…penetrate the things of heaven."

Strepsiades bids Socrates to come down and teach him how to speak because he has "…borrowed money, and my merciless creditors do not leave me a moment's peace; all my goods are at stake." He asks Socrates to "…teach me one of your two methods of reasoning, the one whose object is not to repay anything, and may the gods bear witness, that I am ready to pay any fee you may name."[36]

It is this play that sheds some light on the accusation. The charge accuses Socrates of being what we today would refer to as a lawyer. The "worse cause" would make him a "defense lawyer," protecting people accused of, or actually guilty of, wrong doings. Taken separately, "searches into things under the earth and in heaven," is accusing Socrates of being a "natural philosopher," an astrologer and geologist. In ancient Greece, the common belief was that the stars, sun, and moon were worshiped as gods. To study them as merely anything other than gods would be a disbelief in the gods. These accusations resulted in little action because the Peloponnesian War took priority in the attention of the Athenian people; although, these accusers do not forget him.

Corrupted Youth

There were two young men that were known to associate with Socrates: Alcibiades and Citias. Alcibiades was born to privilege, and after his father died he was raised by his famous uncle, the great leader of Athens, Pericles. Socrates was in a battle where he protected Alcibiades, and Alcibiades returned the favor in another battle:

Whilst he was very young, he was a soldier in the expedition against Potidaea, where Socrates lodged in the same tent with him, and stood next to him in battle. Once there happened a sharp skirmish, in which they both behaved with signal bravery; but Alcibiades receiving a wound, Socrates threw himself before him to defend him, and beyond any question saved him and his arms from the enemy, and so in all justice might have challenged the prize of valour. But the generals appearing eager to adjudge the honour to Alcibiades, because of his rank, Socrates, who desired to increase his thirst after glory of a noble kind, was the first to give evidence for him, and pressed them to crown him, and to decree to him the complete suit of armour. Afterwards, in the battle of Delium, when the Athenians were routed, and Socrates with a few others

was retreating on foot, Alcibiades, who was
on horseback, observing it, would not pass on,
but stayed to shelter him from the danger, and
brought him safe off, though the enemy pressed
hard upon them, and cut off many.[37]

Alcibiades came to political notice in about 420 BC. His
politics seemed to be the cause of the continued fighting
with Sparta. Alcibiades' greatest political opportunity
came in 416 BC, when the Greek cities in Sicily looked
to Athens for help against Syracuse, the largest Greek
city there, which was also an ally of Sparta. Alcibiades
was able to get himself elected general to lead an
expedition against Syracuse, which would essentially
damage the Spartan cause and win the gratitude of the
other Sicilians. Another, but older leader, Nicias was also
elected general to watch over Alcibiades. Because of his
political reputation, preparations began.

In the midst of these preparations all the stone
Hermae in the city of Athens, that is to say the
customary square figures, so common in the
doorways of private houses and temples, had in
one night most of them their fares mutilated.
No one knew who had done it, but large public
rewards were offered to find the authors; and
it was further voted that any one who knew of
any other act of impiety having been committed
should come and give information without fear
of consequences, whether he were citizen, alien,

or slave. The matter was taken up the more seriously, as it was thought to be ominous for the expedition, and part of a conspiracy to bring about a revolution and to upset the democracy.

Information was given accordingly by some resident aliens and body servants, not about the Hermae but about some previous mutilations of other images perpetrated by young men in a drunken frolic, and of mock celebrations of the mysteries, averred to take place in private houses. Alcibiades being implicated in this charge, it was taken hold of by those who could least endure him, because he stood in the way of their obtaining the undisturbed direction of the people, and who thought that if he were once removed the first place would be theirs. These accordingly magnified the matter and loudly proclaimed that the affair of the mysteries and the mutilation of the Hermae were part and parcel of a scheme to overthrow the democracy, and that nothing of all this had been done without Alcibiades; the proofs alleged being the general and undemocratic license of his life and habits.

Alcibiades repelled on the spot the charges in question, and also before going on the expedition, the preparations for which were now complete, offered to stand his trial, that it might be seen whether he was guilty of the acts imputed to him; desiring to be punished if found guilty, but, if acquitted, to take the command. Meanwhile he protested against their receiving slanders against him in his absence, and begged them rather to put him to death at once if he were guilty, and pointed out the imprudence of sending him out at the head of so large an army, with so serious a charge still undecided. But his enemies feared that he would have the army for him if he were tried immediately, and that the people might relent in favour of the man whom they already caressed as the cause of the Argives and some of the Mantineans joining in the expedition, and did their utmost to get this proposition rejected, putting forward other orators who said that he ought at present to sail and not delay the departure of the army, and be tried on his return within a fixed number of days; their plan being to have him sent for and brought home for trial upon some graver charge, which they would the more easily get up in his absence. Accordingly it was decreed that he should sail.

After this the departure for Sicily took place, it being now about midsummer. [38]

A warrant was sworn out for Alcibiades and a ship sent to Syracuse. [39] On the way back, however, Alcibiades jumped ship to avoid prosecution; desertion, evidence of guilt in a charge of sacrilege. But then Alcibiades went even further. He went over to the Spartans. He advised them how to defeat the Athenian expedition in Sicily. The Athenian army and fleet were annihilated. Alcibiades was condemned to death in absentia and his property confiscated.

Alcibiades later began trying to play the Athenians, Spartans, and Persians off of each other. He got the Persians involved, ultimately to the benefit of Sparta, but he also helped the Athenians defeat a Spartan fleet in 410 BC. This enabled him to return to Athens, with all forgiven, for a while. Things soured again with a defeat in 407 BC, and Alcibiades again went into exile. Ironically, his place of exile in 405 BC was where the final battle was fought, Aegospotami, between Athens and Sparta.

In 405 BC both the Athenian and Spartan fleets came into the Straits. For some days they simply maneuvered around each other. In the evening, the fleets separated and the ships were drawn up on the beach for the evening. Although some 100 feet long, such ships could be pulled up on the beach by their own crews. Watching this, Alcibiades walked down to the Athenian camp and warned them that the Spartans might attack as the Athenians were getting out of their ships. The Athenians decided to ignore him. The next day, the Spartans followed the Athenian fleet and attacked as the men were getting out. The Athenian fleet was destroyed. The Spartans sailed directly to Athens, put the city under siege, and starved it into surrender in 404 BC. The war was over.

Alcibiades, like the boy who cried "wolf," was simply no longer someone to believe, even when he was giving good advice. He fled to the Persians and was assassinated in 404 BC, with the agreement of both Athenians and Spartans.[38]

Critias was a leading member of the thirty tyrants that took control of Athens following their defeat in the Peloponnesian War in 404 BC. The Thirty began a purge of citizens who had collaborated with the Athenians during the war. Hundreds were condemned to execution, while thousands more were exiled from Athens. They were overthrown in 403 BC.

Socrates the Accused

These two men, Alcibiades and Critias, turned out to be less than desirable by the Athenians and they blamed Socrates. It did not have to be accurate that Socrates was to blame. It was a convenient excuse to add to the charges that would be brought before the courts against Socrates. In 399 BC Socrates had many accusers; he refers to "older charges" and "later ones." He refers to the older charges as those coming from the older Athenians of his own age, those he grew up with, and the later ones as charges coming from the younger Athenians that have been persuaded by the older Athenians.

> For I have had many accusers, who accused me of old, and their false charges have continued during many years ...
>
> ... But far more dangerous are these, who began when you were children, and took possession of your minds with their falsehoods ... [40]

The older charges, as explained earlier, are as follows:

> Socrates is an evil-doer, and a curious person, who searches into things under the earth and in

heaven, and he makes the worse appear the better cause; and he teaches the aforesaid doctrines to others.[40]

The later charges:

 That Socrates is a doer of evil, and corrupter of the youth, and he does not believe in the gods of the state, and has other new divinities of his own. [40]

In order to understand these charges and the result of them, one needs to consider the prosecuting attorney's strategy. For years now, Socrates has been prophesying and preaching to the Greeks, but the situation in Greece made these complaints seem trivial. The older charges only accused him of studying astronomy, geology, and philosophy, and at worst case he is accused of being a defense attorney that can "…make the worse appear the better cause…" Put all of this together with the new charges and he has a case to take to court. He does not believe in the gods of the state. He has other new divinities of his own. He teaches his doctrine to others. He can persuade people that his cause is the better cause. He studied astronomy and geology, which would be to say that the sun and moon and stars are not gods. All of these things together accuse Socrates of heresy to the belief in the gods. Now consider what this will do to the youth of Greece by looking at the two men that were considered to be Socrates' students, Alcibiades and Critias. Leave Socrates to his ways and he will corrupt and cause all the youth to turn out the same way. So what was he teaching? What was so bad that it required the death penalty?

Like the Babylonian king that destroyed Jerusalem, and the Persian king that invaded Babylon, the Living God, unknown to the Athenians, had chosen Socrates to prophesy and spread his word throughout Athens and perhaps all of Greece. King Nebuchadnezzar was not Jewish. King Cyrus was not Jewish. Socrates was not Jewish. The God of Abraham will use whomever he chooses to fulfill his desires. From the time Socrates was a child, God spoke to him and used him. These are the last days of the Old Testament, the days of the last prophets. Here Socrates now stands in the midst of the Areopagus, where Paul will stand some 450 years later, facing these same charges of introducing a foreign God.

Socrates was executed in the year 399 BC. There are 400 years between the Old and New Testaments, known as the 400 years of silence. It leaves to question what would have happened if Socrates was not silenced. Let us take a closer look at Socrates and ask a few more questions.

In attempting to gather accurate information about Socrates, scholars face a specific problem. The problem (widely referred to as the Socratic problem) is due to the following circumstances:

The primary sources relating to Socrates amount to the writing of four men: Xenophon, Plato, Aristotle, and Aristophanes. The information coming from these sources was written in artistic and philosophical styles that imply a level of creativity or imagination upon the part of the writer.

Therefore, the primary source for the life of Socrates comes without any claims of historical accuracy. And since there are no known writings by Socrates, historians are faced with the challenge of reading between the lines of the various texts that come from these men to create an accurate and consistent account of the historical Socrates.

In general, Plato is viewed as the most reliable source of information about Socrates' life and philosophy. Therefore, most classicists claim that any description of Socrates must agree with what Plato wrote in his dialogues. However, information about Socrates cannot rely upon that source alone. If Plato were the only existing source of information about Socrates, there would be no reason to think that Socrates was an actual, historical figure. Without further evidence, Socrates could merely be chalked up as a spokesperson for Plato's philosophical agenda. Instead, those that study Socrates must use the testimony of Xenophon and Aristotle (and some times alongside a careful reading of Aristophanes' *The Clouds*) to compare to the portrayal of Socrates within the dialogues of Plato.

Who was Plato and why is his description of Socrates so important? It is said that Plato was Socrates' student. The question is whether this is true: Do men claim that Plato was the student of Socrates because he wrote about

Socrates? Or did Plato write about Socrates because he was Socrates' student?

First, a definition of what is meant by the word "student" is needed. The dictionary defines a student as "a person formally engaged in learning" and "any person who studies, investigates, or examines thoughtfully." If we look into the writings of Plato, particularly the *Apology* [translated by Benjamin Jowett], we find that he was not considered a student by Socrates, and never received lessons from Socrates. In the *Apology*, Socrates tells us:

> For the truth is that I have no regular disciples [Students]. But if any one likes to come and hear me while I am pursuing my mission, whether he be young or old, he may freely come. Nor do I converse with those who pay only, and not with those who do not pay; but anyone, whether he be rich or poor, may ask and answer me and listen to my words; and whether he turns out to be a bad man or a good one, that cannot be justly laid to my charge, as I never taught him anything. And if anyone says that he has ever learned or heard anything from me in private which all the world has not heard, I should like you to know that he is speaking an untruth.[40]

We also find in the *Apology* that Socrates does not consider Plato to be his successor:

{ And now, Athenians, I am not going to argue for my own sake, as you may think, but for yours, that you may not sin against the God, or lightly reject his boon by condemning me, who am his gift to you. For if you kill me you will not easily find another like me ... [40] }

If Socrates had trained Plato, surely he would have acknowledged Plato as his successor, ready to replace him. It is more likely that Plato was an admirer of Socrates and followed him around, listening to him speak as often as possible. Plato falls into the second definition of student, "a person who studies, investigates, or examines thoughtfully," but he was clearly not "formally engaged in learning" from Socrates. By following this thought, Plato was most likely impressed enough with Socrates to study him and write in a manner that emulates Socrates.

Clearly Plato did not write about Socrates because he was Socrates' formal student. Therefore the first explanation must be true. "Men claim that Plato was the student of Socrates because he wrote about Socrates." But is this a sound statement? Can we call someone Socrates' student merely because he writes about him? Let's look at this argument and see if it is valid.

> Premise: Anyone that wrote about Socrates was Socrates' student.
>
> Premise: Plato wrote about Socrates.
>
> Conclusion: Plato was Socrates Student.

This seems valid, but it is not. The first premise is not

true, therefore the conclusion is false. An example of why it is false is simple. What about Xenophon (*Memorabilia*) or Aristophanes (*The Clouds*)? They also wrote about Socrates, but are not considered Socrates' students. Aristotle was not even alive during Socrates' time, yet he also writes about Socrates. For that matter, I am writing about Socrates. Does that make me his student? It would therefore stand to reason that an author can write about someone without being the student of that person. He can write about someone and be an observer or a friend, for example. Then there is the question, did Plato write "about" Socrates, or only in the manner of Socrates. Can we trust what Plato tells us is Socrates, or did Plato borrow Socrates' name and manner of conversation only? Did Plato include just enough facts about Socrates to make us believe that everything was true? It is commonly accepted by scholars that the later writings of Plato are embellishments using the name of Socrates only, so why believe that all his writings are complete facts? How can we separate fact from embellishment? We were not there at the time, and therefore can not separate them. We can only pick and choose, and then argue that we are right and someone else is wrong.

Another question must be asked. If Plato was taught by Socrates, either directly or through observation, and he continued the teachings of Socrates without diverging from the technique and subject matter, would he not be guilty of the same crimes as Socrates? Would he not face the same penalties? Would the Athenian government allow Plato to build a school and teach others what Socrates had taught him?

I want to answer these questions by looking at another person in history that fell to the same fate as Socrates. This person was born 400 years later in a town called Bethlehem. He too was accused of corrupting the minds of the people, and was sentenced to death. His name was Jesus the Nazarene. Jesus had twelve disciples that he taught in his ways. And these men continued in the ways of Jesus after his death. Eleven of these men were captured and executed in an effort to silence them. So is it possible that Plato continued in the ways of Socrates? Or did he embellish the stories to protect himself from the chastisements of Socrates' accusers? If embellish is an incorrect word to use, perhaps Plato chose to leave out the things that would get him into trouble and use Socrates as a spokesperson for his own agendas. If either of these can be true, then we must ask ourselves what was Socrates' true goal. What was he trying to do and how would he want to be remembered? What did he actually teach and are the modern philosophers teaching the same thing, or just using the same methods to teach their own philosophies?

In the writings of Plato, Xenophon, and Aristophanes, we see that Socrates was a man of meager means. In Aristophanes' play *The Clouds* he writes:

> "Bah! The wretches! I know them; you mean those quacks with pale faces, those barefoot fellows, such as that miserable Socrates and Chaerephon?"[36]

This is interesting in itself because Xenophon, Socrates' friend, wrote about Socrates in the *Memorabilia,* Book I, section VI; telling us about Socrates' meager lifestyle. This is a dialogue between Socrates and Antiphon.

Antiphon says: "Why, Socrates, I always thought it was expected of students of philosophy to grow in happiness daily; but you seem to have reaped other fruits from your philosophy. At any rate, you exist, I do not say live, in a style such as no slave serving under a master would put up with. Your meat and your drink are of the cheapest sort, and as to clothes, you cling to one wretched cloak which serves you for summer and winter alike; and so you go the whole year round, without shoes to your feet or a shirt to your back."[41]

Antiphon would go on to say that Socrates is not one for taking or making money, as does Plato, which is where the play strays from the truth of Socrates. The play did, however, describe Socrates correctly by calling him a barefoot fellow.

So what was it that Socrates was preaching? He tells us in Plato's dialogue of the *Apology.* Socrates says:

For this is the command of God, as I would have you know; and I believe that to this day no greater good has ever happened in the state than my service to the God. For I do nothing but go

> about persuading you all, old and young alike, not to take thought for your persons and your properties, but first and chiefly to care about the greatest improvement of the soul.[40]

Xenophon also describes the reaction of those listening at the time:

> As they listened to these words the judges murmured their dissent, some as disbelieving what was said, and others out of simple envy that Socrates should actually receive from heaven more than they themselves … [34]

Socrates seems to be placing himself on a high pedestal to be able to hear directly from God. Does Socrates claim to hear the voice of Apollo? He does not name the God that he is hearing from, but he mentions the Oracle of Delphi and so Apollo is assumed to be the god that Socrates refers to. But Socrates did not go to Delphi; it was his friend Chaerephon that went there. In writing about this case, it is possible for Plato to misdirect Socrates' statements because of his own beliefs and interpretations.

Apollo is not a new divinity, along with the many other gods of the Greek cities, Zeus, Hera, Hades, Ares, Demeter, Poseidon, Hestia, Artemis, Dionysus, Hermes, Aphrodite, and others. It is more likely that Socrates is referring to a God with no name, a God not recognized by the Greeks at that time, and that this God is the new divinity he is charged with introducing. I will not suggest that Socrates was a monotheist, since he admits to recognizing the gods of Greece. However, it is not likely that Socrates would have been accused of introducing a new divinity if he was referring to Apollo. Some scholars will excuse the lack of a proper name as being normal for ancient Greeks. They even suggest that the Jews do not speak the name of the God of Abraham and Isaac because the true pronunciation was actually forgotten. Opinions vary and none can be proven, only suggested.

So here is a valid argument:

Premise: Apollo is not a new divinity to the Greek city of Athens.

Premise: Socrates is accused of introducing a new Divinity.

Conclusion: Apollo is not the divinity that Socrates is accused of introducing.

So what "new divinity" was Socrates introducing? This is the most serious accusation brought before the court. This is the accusation which was most likely the cause of the trial.

It is made very clear by the following passage in the *Apology* what Socrates' mission in life was: to care about the greatest improvement of the soul.

> For this is the command of God, as I would have you know; and I believe that to this day no greater good has ever happened in the state than my service to the God. For I do nothing but go

about persuading you all, old and young alike, not to take thought for your persons or your properties, but first and chiefly to care about the greatest improvement of the soul. I tell you that virtue is not given by money, but that from virtue comes money and every other good of man, public as well as private. This is my teaching, and if this is the doctrine which corrupts the youth, my influence is ruinous indeed. But if any one says that this is not my teaching, he is speaking an untruth.

I am that gadfly which God has given the state and all day long and in all places am always fastening upon you, arousing and persuading and reproaching you…

…if I had been like other men, I should not have neglected all my own concerns, or patiently seen the neglect of them during all these years, and have been doing yours, coming to you individually, like a father or elder brother, exhorting you to regard virtue; this I say, would not be like human nature.[40]

Socrates describes his mission as going to individuals and exhorting them. He is reporting to them the counsels of heaven. Much like the prophets of Israel did, Socrates is doing the same thing in Greece. There are a couple of places in Plato's *Apology* that Socrates claims to prophesy. After he has been sentenced, he says to those that have condemned him:

{ And now, O men who have condemned me, I would fain prophesy to you; for I am about to die, and that is the hour in which men are gifted with prophetic power. And I prophesy to you who are my murderers that immediately after my death punishment far heavier than you have inflicted on me will surely await you.

Men of Athens, I honor and love you; but I shall obey God rather than you ... [40] }

Socrates was one of the last Prophets of the Living God during the Old Testament times. He was executed and the 400 years of silence begins. Some time after his execution the Greeks began to think about what Socrates had been teaching. Was there actually another God that they had not been worshiping? Could they be missing out on some blessings? Who was this God of Socrates? What is he called?

Without the answers to these questions, they made a decision. They built an altar to this "Unknown God" and began to worship him. It did not matter how many gods they were unaware of, because this altar would cover them all. It is this altar that Paul finds in his travels and discusses with the Stoic and Epicurean philosophers in Athens. Paul is introducing them to the God they have been worshiping and did not know. He even quotes part of a poem from Epimenides, a sixth century BC Greek philosopher-poet that wrote a famous poem where Minos addresses Zeus:

> They fashioned a tomb for thee, O holy and high one—
>   The Cretans, always liars, evil beasts, idle bellies!
>   But thou art not dead: thou livest and abidest forever,
>   *For in thee we live and move and have our being.*[42]

Minos is claiming that Zeus is immortal and that the people from Crete, the Cretans, claim that he is mortal by fashioning a tomb for him. He is calling the Cretans liars for calling Zeus mortal. Minos says that Zeus is not dead, but livest and abidest forever. Minos is the son of Zeus and the mythical king of Crete. So for Minos to say it was because of Zeus that "we (at least him and his brothers) live and move and have our being," he would be correct. Paul quotes this poem and says that it is because of the "Unknown God" who created all things that "we live and move and have our being." Are we like these Greeks, worshiping blindly and hoping we cover all our bases? Do we create an Alter to an unknown god and hope our sins will be overlooked, not knowing or caring what god we worship?

Summary

The living God is a jealous God who created all things. All He requires is that we worship Him and give Him praise. From the days of the Old Testament prophets we have been told, "Turn back to God and worship Him." There is a famous question that can be answered now: "What is the purpose of life?" By looking into the history of Israel we can find this answer:

To praise and worship God.

> Make a joyful noise unto the LORD, all ye lands. Serve the LORD with gladness: come before his presence with singing. Know ye that the LORD he is God: it is he that hath made us, and not we ourselves; we are his people, and the sheep of his pasture. Enter into his gates with thanksgiving, and into his courts with praise: be thankful unto him, and bless his name.
>
> Psalms 100:1–4 (KJV)

> … worship the LORD your God; it is he who will deliver you from the hand of all your enemies.
>
> 2 Kings 17:39

From the very beginning, and throughout history, we are

told how important praise and worship is to God. The Bible tells us of three archangels.

The first is Michael, the angel of war, who was always sent by God to fight against the enemy of His people:

> But the prince of the Persian kingdom resisted me twenty-one days. Then Michael, one of the chief princes, came to help me, because I was detained there with the king of Persia.
>
> Daniel 10:13 (NIV)

> …but first I will tell you what is written in the Book of Truth. No one supports me against them except Michael, your prince.
>
> Daniel 10:21 (NIV)

> At that time Michael, the great prince *who protects your people*, will arise. There will be a time of distress such as has not happened from the beginning of nations until then. But at that time your people—everyone whose name is found written in the book—will be delivered.
>
> Daniel 12:1 (NIV)

> And there was war in heaven. Michael and his angels fought against the dragon, and the dragon and his angels fought back.
>
> Revelation 12:7 (NIV)

The second archangel is Gabriel, the messenger angel, who was always giving messages to God's people.

> And I heard a man's voice from the Ulai calling, "Gabriel, tell this man the meaning of the vision."
>
> Daniel 8:16 (NIV)
>
> While I was still in prayer, Gabriel, the man I had seen in the earlier vision, came to me in swift flight about the time of the evening sacrifice. He instructed me and said to me, "Daniel, I have now come to give you insight and understanding."
>
> Daniel 9:21–22 (NIV)
>
> The angel answered, "I am Gabriel. I stand in the presence of God, and I have been sent to speak to you and to tell you this good news.
>
> Luke 1:19 (NIV)

The third archangel is Lucifer, the praise and worship angel that was cast out of heaven.

> And there was war in heaven. Michael and his angels fought against the dragon, and the dragon and his angels fought back. But he was not strong enough, and they lost their place in heaven. The great dragon was hurled down—that ancient serpent called the devil, or Satan, who leads the

whole world astray. He was hurled to the earth, and his angels with him.

Revelation 12:7–9 (NIV)

How you have fallen from heaven, O morning star, son of the dawn! You have been cast down to the earth, you who once laid low the nations! You said in your heart, "I will ascend to heaven; I will raise my throne above the stars of God; I will sit enthroned on the mount of assembly, on the utmost heights of the sacred mountain. I will ascend above the tops of the clouds; I will make myself like the Most High." But you are brought down to the grave, to the depths of the pit.

Isaiah 14:12–15 (NIV)

Lucifer and his host of angels were called the morning stars in Isaiah 14. In Job 38: 4–7, God says to Job:

Where were you when I laid the earth's foundation? Tell me, if you understand. Who marked off its dimensions? Surely you know! Who stretched a measuring line across it? On what were its footings set, or who laid its cornerstone—*while the morning stars sang together and all the angels shouted for joy?*

Job 38:4–7 (NIV)

This shows the angels, including Satan, were present before the foundations of the earth were laid. The time when God "created the heavens" and "the earth" is when all the morning stars sang together, and all the angels shouted for joy. And Satan was the leader of these singers and shouters, the praise and worship team.

Each of these archangels, Michael, Gabriel, and Lucifer, was the leading angel of one third of the host of all angels in heaven. We are told that when Lucifer was cast out of heaven, a third of the host of angels was cast out with him.

When these angels were cast out of heaven, there were no angels to praise and worship God. Man was created to fill that gap, to replace Lucifer and the other angels. No wonder Satan hates man so much. We were created to replace Satan, to praise and worship God. When God's people turned their backs on Him and refused to praise and worship Him, He devastated them by sending in their enemies.

> "O House of Israel," declares the LORD, "I am bringing a distant nation against you—an ancient and enduring nation, a people whose language you do not know, whose speech you do not understand. Their quivers are like an open grave; all of them are mighty warriors. They will devour your harvests and food, devour your sons and daughters; they will devour your flocks and herds, devour your vines and fig trees. With the sword they will destroy the fortified cities in which you trust.
>
> Yet even in those days, declares the LORD, I

will not destroy you completely. And when the people ask, "Why has the LORD our God done all this to us?" you will tell them, "as you have forsaken me and served foreign gods in your own land, so now you will serve foreigners in a land not your own."

Jeremiah 5:15–19 (NIV)

The Legend of the Unknown God is simple. God seeks a nation, a people that will praise and worship Him. The people of Israel and Judah turned their backs on him and began to worship false gods and practice sorcery. A trip through the pages of history reveals the cry of the Lord to His people and His punishment for their rebellion, he took away their kingdoms. Today they still fight with their neighboring countries.

The United States is a country founded on the freedom to praise and worship God, but today has turned its back on him much like Israel. We need a leader that will turn the United States back to worshiping and praising God. Only then will this country become strong and prosper once more.

In the book of Exodus chapter 20 is found the laws of Moses, most commonly referred to as the Ten Commandments.

1. "You shall have no other gods before me.

2. "You shall not make for yourself an idol in the form of anything in heaven above or on the earth beneath or in the waters below. You shall not bow down to

them or worship them; for I, the Lord your God, am a jealous God, punishing the children for the sin of the fathers to the third and fourth generation of those who hate me, but showing love to a thousand {generations} of those who love me and keep my commandments.

3. "You shall not misuse the name of the Lord your God, for the Lord will not hold anyone guiltless who misuses his name.

4. "Remember the Sabbath day by keeping it holy. Six days you shall labor and do all your work, but the seventh day is a Sabbath to the Lord your God. On it you shall not do any work, neither you, nor your son or daughter, nor your manservant or maidservant, nor your animals, nor the alien within your gates. For in six days the Lord made the heavens and the earth, the sea, and all that is in them, but he rested on the seventh day. Therefore the LORD blessed the Sabbath day and made it holy.

5. "Honor your father and your mother, so that you may live long in the land the LORD your God is giving you.

6. "You shall not murder.

7. "You shall not commit adultery.

8. "You shall not steal.

9. "You shall not give false testimony against your neighbor.

10. "You shall not covet your neighbor's house. You shall

not covet your neighbor's wife, or his manservant or maidservant, his ox or donkey, or anything that belongs to your neighbor."

I draw your attention to the first two commandments.

1. "You shall have no other gods before me."

2. "You shall not make for yourself an idol in the form of anything in heaven above or on the earth beneath or in the waters below. You shall not bow down to them or worship them; for I, the LORD your God, am a jealous God, punishing the children for the sin of the fathers to the third and fourth generation of those who hate me, but showing love to a thousand {generations} of those who love me and keep my commandments."

I like the message that Ray Comfort and Kirk Cameron are putting out. I want to emphasize that message here. Visit their website at *www.livingwaters.com.* The people of the United States have created false gods and are worshiping them. In their minds they say: "My god is a forgiving god and would not send me to hell for this or for that…" They create a god to suit their lifestyle, a false god, a god in their own image. Their god accepts small lies and minor thefts. Their god accepts lust and corruption, adultery and dishonoring their parents. But the Living God is a jealous God that will punish those that worship false gods and that sin against his commandments. He is the same yesterday, today, and forever. He destroyed the kingdoms of Israel and Judah; he can destroy the nation of the United States as well. He requires a blood sacrifice for the redemption of sin and sent his son Jesus to die for us on a cross and bear our sins through the shedding of His blood.

In the words of Socrates:

> For this is the command of God, as I would have you know; and I believe that to this day no greater good has ever happened in the state than my service to the God. For I do nothing but go about persuading you all, old and young alike, not to take thought for your persons or your properties, but first and chiefly to care about the greatest improvement of the soul.[40]

Turn back to God. You can not create and worship a god that fits your lifestyle and expect the Living God to welcome you into heaven. You must create a lifestyle that fits the desires of the Living God. Fulfill the purpose of life: honor, praise, and worship the Living God. Accept the blood sacrifice of Jesus Christ His son as your savior and the redeemer of your sins. Then when you stand before him on the Day of Judgment, he will not say to you, "Depart from me, I never knew you." But instead Jesus will say, "Welcome thou good and faithful servant, enter into the kingdom of Heaven." The Living God is the God that Paul and Socrates introduced to the Athenians as the "Unknown God" and the Living God is the God today that pleads for us to turn back to Him.

We, in the United States, have the ability to elect our government officials. We need to elect those that will honor our nation by honoring the Living God. Remember the prophetic words of Jeremiah to Judah:

> 'I am bringing a distant nation against you—an ancient and enduring nation, a people whose language you do not know, whose speech you do not understand. Their quivers are like an open grave; all of them are mighty warriors. They will devour your harvests and food, devour your sons and daughters; they will devour your flocks and herds, devour your vines and fig trees. With the sword they will destroy the fortified cities in which you trust.
>
> Yet even in those days,' declares the LORD, 'I will not destroy you completely. And when the people ask, 'Why has the LORD our God done all this to us?' you will tell them, 'as you have forsaken me and served foreign gods in your own land, so now you will serve foreigners in a land not your own.'"
>
> Jeremiah 5:15–19 (NIV)

If we compare the countries we know today with the Empires of the ancient world of the eighth through fifth centuries BC, we see that the Assyrian Empire was made up of the following countries: Iraq, Iran, and parts of Lebanon, Syria, and Jordan. These are the people that invaded the Kingdom of Israel and exiled the people from Samaria. Then the Babylonian Empire rose up and took over the Assyrian Empire and invaded Judah, exiling the people to Babylon. Then the Persian Empire shows up and takes over. Some of the countries today that made up the Persian Empire which invaded the Babylonian Empire are: Turkey, Armenia, Azerbaijan, Tajikistan, Kyrgyzstan, Afghanistan, Turkmenistan, Uzbekistan, Pakistan, and parts of Jordan.

It should not surprise us that the people we are having troubles with today are from the same areas that the people of Israel and Judah had problems with more than 2,500 years ago. God used them to punish Israel and Judah for turning their backs on Him and worshiping foreign gods. He can certainly use them today!

Don't think that the United States is immune to God's anger. He blessed this nation and he can destroy it. We took him out of our schools and forced our governments to turn their backs on him by not acknowledging him. The term "Separation of Church and State" originally meant that the government could not establish a state or national religion. Now it means that the government can not support any religion that recognizes God. Satanic worship is also a religion, and if our government does not honor the Living God, then they honor Satan. It's like the phrase, "If you're not with me, then you are against me." This is the cry of God to our government: "Turn back to God, because if you are not for me, you are against me." Put God back into the government and back into the schools.

The wrath of God is being revealed from heaven against all the godlessness and wickedness of men who suppress the truth by their wickedness, since what may be known about God is plain to them, because God has made it plain to them. For since the creation of the world God's invisible qualities—his eternal power and divine nature—have been clearly seen, being understood from what has been made, so that men are without excuse.

For although they knew God, they neither glorified him as God nor gave thanks to him, but their thinking became futile and their foolish hearts were darkened. Although they claimed to be wise, they became fools and exchanged the glory of the immortal God for images made to look like mortal man and birds and animals and reptiles.

Therefore God gave them over in the sinful desires of their hearts to sexual impurity for the degrading of their bodies with one another. They exchanged the truth of God for a lie, and worshiped and served created things rather than the Creator—who is forever praised. Amen.

Because of this, God gave them over to shameful lusts. Even their women exchanged natural relations for unnatural ones. In the same way the men also abandoned natural relations with women and were inflamed with lust for one another. Men committed indecent acts with other men, and received in themselves the due penalty for their perversion.

Furthermore, since they did not think it worthwhile to retain the knowledge of God, he gave them over to a depraved mind to do what ought not to be done. They have become filled with every kind of wickedness, evil, greed and depravity. They are full of envy, murder, strife, deceit and malice. They are gossips, slanderers, God-haters, insolent, arrogant and boastful; they invent ways of doing evil; they disobey their parents; they are senseless, faithless, heartless, ruthless. Although they know God's righteous decree that those who do such things deserve death, they not only continue to do these very things but also approve of those who practice them.

Romans 1:20–32 (NIV)

How can a church support the homosexual lifestyle by allowing homosexuality to continue among their congregations? Some churches have welcomed homosexuality into the church and have approved of their practice. It is true that God loves the homosexual person but he despises their lifestyle. A church can love the person but must not approve of their lifestyle. The church should preach against this perversion and attempt to turn the homosexual back to God. It seems to be about the almighty dollar. The more people in the seats, the more money in the plate! God will bless the church that worships Him.

"Oh, but my god is not like that, he would never punish me. I am a good person!" Your god is not the Living God. Your god is the god of your lifestyle, a god that accepts your sins and laughs at them. The Living God will surely pass judgment on you. "For the wages of sin is death; but the gift of God is eternal life through Jesus Christ our Lord" (Romans 6:23, NIV).

Jesus Christ died for our sins and became our blood sacrifice. It is through him that we are forgiven and find favor in the eyes of God. Turn back to him!

This is the legend of the Unknown God!

(Endnotes)

1   Notes to the Text. Thompson Chain Reference Study Bible, NIV, Daniel 1:1

2   "Battle of Carchemish—Britannica online encyclopedia," 28 July 2008,<http://www.britannica.com/EBchecked/topic/95348/Battle-of-Carchemish>

3   "Chronicle concerning the early years of Nebuchadnezzar II." Jerusalem Chronicles, (Abc 5), Reverse side, lines 11–13, A.K. Grayson, Assyrian and Babylonian Chronicles (1975) and Jean-Jacques Glassner, Mesopotamian Chronicles (Atlanta, 2004), June 2008, <http://www.livius.org/cg-cm/chronicles/abc5/jerusalem.html>

4   Thompson Chain Reference Study Bible, NIV, 2 Kings 25:8–12

5   Thompson Chain Reference Study Bible, NIV, 2 Kings 25:25

6   Thompson Chain Reference Study Bible, NIV, Daniel 2

7   Thompson Chain Reference Study Bible, NIV, Daniel 3

8   Thompson Chain Reference Study Bible, NIV, Isaiah 45

9   "The Baldwin Project, Stories of the East from Herodotus," Alfred J. Church, 28 July 2008, The Birth and Bringing up of Cyrus, <http://www.mainlesson.com/display.php?author=church&book=storieseast&story=birth>

10 "Nitocris Princess of Egypt," 2 August 2008, <http://www.american-pictures.com/genealogy/persons/per04127.htm#o>

11 "Amel-Marduk," 30 July 2008,<http://www.livius.org/ne-nn/nebuchadnezzar/amel-marduk.html>

12 "The Chronicles concerning the third year of Neriglissar" The Chronicle concerning year three of Neriglissar (Abc 6), 1 August 2008, < http://www.livius.org/cg-cm/chronicles/abc6/neriglissar.html>

13 "Niticris Princess of Babylon," 2 August 2008, < http://www.american-pictures.com/genealogy/persons/per01995.htm#o>

14 "Cyrus takes Babylon, the Chronicles of Nabonidus," the sixth year (550/549 bc), 2 August 2008, < http://www.livius.org/ct-cz/cyrus_I/babylon02.html#Chronicle%20of%20Nabonidus>

15 "The Baldwin Project: Stories of the East from Herodotus," The Story of King Croesus, Chapter 1, Alfred J. Church, 3 January 2008, < http://www.mainlesson.com/display.php?author=church&book=storieseast&story=king&PHPSESSID=100922ed72033e51ba9ab84c32ae10ef>

16   "The Baldwin Project: Stories of the East from Herodotus," Croesus, Wishing to make war against the Persians, consulteth the Oracles, Alfred J. Church, 4 January 2008, <http://www.mainlesson.com/display.php?author=church&book=storieseast&story=war

17   "The Baldwin Project: Stories of the East from Herodotus," Croesus is saved from death, Alfred J. Church, 4 January 2008, < http://www.mainlesson.com/display.php?author=church&book=storieseast&story=saved>

18   "Cyrus takes Babylon, the Chronicles of Nabonidus," the seventeenth year (539/538 bc), 2 August 2008, <http://www.livius.org/ct-cz/cyrus_I/babylon02.html#Chronicle%20of%20Nabonidus>

19   "Cyrus takes Babylon, (530 bc)," The Cyrus Cylinder, lines 30–40, 8 January 2008, <http://www.livius.org/ct-cz/cyrus_I/babylon05.html>

20   Thompson Chain Reference Study Bible, NIV, Ezra chapter 4

21   Antiquities of the Jews–Book XI, chapter 2, Flavius Josephus, 12 February 2008, <http://www.sacred-texts.com/jud/josephus/ant-11.htm>

22   "The Internet Classics Archive, The History of Herodotus," Herodotus, translated by George Rawlinson, 2 August 2008, <http://classics.mit.edu/Herodotus/history.3.iii.html>

23   "Complete Pythagoras," Iamblichus, Interpreted by Kenneth Sylvan Guthrie, 1920–accessed 12 December 2007, <http://www.completepythagoras.net >

24   "The works of Flavius Josephus: The Antiquities of Josephus, The wars of Josephus, The life of Josephus, and Against Apion by Josephus" Book 1: Flavius Josephus against Apion, Paragraph #22, by Flavius Josephus, Translated by William Whiston, 2 August 2008, <http://www.earlychristianwritings.com/text/josephus/apion-1.htm>

25   "The Internet Classics Archive, The History of Herodotus," Herodotus, translated by George Rawlinson, Book 3–Thalia, 3.80, 2 August 2008, <http://classics.mit.edu/Herodotus/history.3.iii.html>

26   "Antiquities of the Jews, Book XI," Flavius Josephus, Translated by William Whiston 1737, 13 November 2008, <http://www.sacred-texts.com/jud/josephus/ant-11.htm>

27   Thompson Chain Reference Study Bible, NIV, Ezra Chapter 6:2–12

28   "The Ionian Revolt," Logan Nielsen, 3 August 2008, <http://ehistory.osu.edu/world/articles/ArticleView.cfm?AID=19>

29   "The Internet Classics Archive, The History of Herodotus," Herodotus, translated by George Rawlinson, Book 5–Terpsichore, 2 December 2007, <http://classics.mit.edu/Herodotus/history.5.v.html>

30 "The Internet Classics Archive, The History of Herodotus," Herodotus, translated by George Rawlinson Book 7–Polymnia, 2 December 2007, < http://classics.mit.edu/Herodotus/history.7.vii.html>

31 "The Internet Classics Archive, The History of Herodotus," Herodotus, translated by George Rawlinson Book 8–Urania, 3 December 2007, <http://classics.mit.edu/Herodotus/history.8.viii.html>

32 "The Internet Classics Archive, Phaedo by Plato," Phaedo–in the prison of Socrates, Translated by Benjamin Jowett, 5 September 2007, <.http://www.davemckay.co.uk/philosophy/plato/plato.php?name=phaedo&trns=jowett>

33 "The Internet Classics Archive, Apology by Plato," Apology, Translated by Benjamin Jowett, 5 September 2007, <http://classics.mit.edu/Plato/apology.html>

34 "Xenophen, the Apology of Socrates," Xenophen, Translated by H. G. Dakyns, 15 December 2007, <http://www.davemckay.co.uk/philosophy/xenophon/xenophon.php?name=apology>

35 "Plato, Apology," Plato, Translated by Benjamin Jowett, 5 September 2007, <http://www.davemckay.co.uk/philosophy/plato/plato.php?name=apology&trns=jowett>

36 "The Internet Classics Archives, The Clouds by Aristophanes," Aristophanes, 22 November 2007, <http://classics.mit.edu/Aristophanes/clouds.html>

37 "The Internet Classics Archives, Alcibiades by Plutarch," Translated by John Dryden, 4 August 2008, <http://classics.mit.edu/Plutarch/alcibiad.html>

38 "The Internet Classics Archives, The history of the Peloponnesian War, by Thucydides," book six, chapter XVIII, 4 August 2008, <http://classics.mit.edu/Thucydides/pelopwar.6.sixth.html>

39 "The Internet Classics Archives, The history of the Peloponnesian War, by Thucydides," book six, chapter XIX, 4 August 2008, <http://classics.mit.edu/Thucydides/pelopwar.6.sixth.html>

40 "Plato, Apology," Plato, Translated by Benjamin Jowett, 5 September 2007, <http://www.davemckay.co.uk/philosophy/plato/plato.php?name=apology&trns=jowett>

41 "Memorabilia, Book I, Section IV," Xenophon, translated by H.G. Dakyns, 3 September 2007,< http://www.davemckay.co.uk/philosophy/xenophon/xenophon.php?name=memorabilia.01.04>

42 "Epimenides, Wikipedia the free encyclopedia," 4 August 2008,< http://en.wikipedia.org/wiki/Epimenides>